The LIFE of JOSEPH

CLARENCE SEXTON

CROWN
CHRISTIAN
PUBLICATIONS
Royal Reading

The LIFE of JOSEPH

CLARENCE SEXTON

FIRST EDITION
COPYRIGHT
AUGUST 2004

CROWN
CHRISTIAN
PUBLICATIONS
Royal Reading

PILLAR
AND GROUND
OF THE TRUTH
CHURCH PLANTING AND
SUNDAY SCHOOL SERIES

THE LIFE OF JOSEPH

Copyright © 2004
Crown Christian Publications
Powell, Tennessee 37849
ISBN: 1-58981-234-4

Printed in the United States of America

Dedication

This study of the life of Joseph is dedicated to the wonderful young people of the Temple Baptist Church. One of the great joys of my life is to watch them grow in the grace and knowledge of the Lord Jesus Christ and follow Him.

Contents

Chapter One

THE LIFE OF JOSEPH

"GOD MEANT IT UNTO GOOD"

he life of Joseph is one of the most beautiful lives ever lived. There are few characters in the Bible as glorious to study as the man Joseph. As we begin this study, let us familiarize ourselves with the highlights of Joseph's life.

SOLD INTO SLAVERY

We begin reading about Joseph in the thirty-seventh chapter of the book of Genesis. Joseph was a son of Jacob, whose name had been changed to Israel. The Bible says in Genesis 37:3, *"Now Israel loved Joseph more than all his children, because he was the son of his old age: and he made him a coat of many colours."* Joseph was hated by his brothers because he was his father's favorite son.

When Joseph was seventeen years old, he was sent by Jacob to check on his brothers. The Word of God says in Genesis 37:18, *"And when they saw him afar off, even before he came near unto them, they conspired against him to slay him."* They stripped Joseph of his beautiful robe and cast him into a pit. Instead of taking his life, they decided to sell him to the Ishmeelite merchants for twenty pieces of silver. Joseph was sold into slavery.

> *Joseph was better off in Egypt in the care of God than he was in Canaan among his brothers who despised and envied him.*

With shock we declare, "What a tragedy that Joseph was sent out by his father to visit his brethren and they sold him into slavery!" Yes, but Joseph said in Genesis 50:20, *"God meant it unto good."*

We may say, "What a horrible coincidence! How could such a terrible coincidence take place? As Joseph's brothers were thinking about what they were going to do with him, it just so happened that across the horizon came merchantmen traveling down to Egypt." Yes, but we know that *"God meant it unto good."*

God's ways are not our ways, but God knows all things. Joseph's brothers were so hard-hearted that they sat and ate their lunch while Joseph called out for mercy from the pit. They sold Joseph. They took the coat his father had made him, tore it, and covered it with blood. They made it appear to their father that a wild beast had slain Joseph.

Jacob certainly thought, "If I had not sent him, if I had not asked him to go, he would never have been killed by a wild beast." No doubt Jacob blamed himself for Joseph's death. Those heartless brothers lived with that lie until they came face to face with Joseph many years later.

Let us follow Joseph to Egypt. The Bible says in Genesis 37:36, *"And the Midianites sold him into Egypt unto Potiphar, an officer of Pharaoh's, and captain of the guard."* Joseph was sold again.

The Word of God says in Genesis 29:1-2, *"And Joseph was brought down to Egypt; and Potiphar, an officer of Pharaoh, captain of the guard, an Egyptian, bought him of the hands of the Ishmeelites, which had brought him down thither. And the LORD was with Joseph."*

BETTER IN EGYPT

Joseph was better off in Egypt in the care of God than he was in Canaan among his brothers who despised and envied him.

The Word of God says in Genesis 39:3, *"And his master saw that the LORD was with him, and that the LORD made all that he did to prosper in his hand."*

Do you know that God is with you? No matter what men do to you or choose to say about you, if you walk with God, God will honor your life. He will bless you and take care of you.

Joseph served in the house of Potiphar. However, there came a time when Potiphar's wife set her eyes on Joseph. When she attempted to seduce Joseph, he testified in Genesis 39:9, *"There is none greater in this house than I; neither hath he kept back any thing from me but thee, because thou art his wife: how then can I do this great wickedness, and sin against God?"*

Our sin is inescapable!

God was all-sufficient to Joseph. Joseph was not saying, "Look, you're another man's wife, and I'm not going to commit this sin with you." Joseph declared, *"How then can I do this great wickedness, and sin against God?"*

11

What happened? Joseph ran away from Potiphar's wife. He left his coat, but he kept his character. Then, from Potiphar's house, he was sent to prison. The Bible says in Genesis 39:21, *"But the LORD was with Joseph."*

BETTER IN PRISON

This is hard to imagine, but Joseph was in the lap of luxury in Potiphar's house. He had everything a man could imagine. Potiphar was quite a noble man in Egypt. However, Joseph was better off in prison with his character and integrity than he was living in the lap of luxury in Potiphar's house. The foundation of Joseph's character was his faith in God.

When we come to the end of ourselves, then our sweet, precious Lord can make Himself truly known to us.

The Bible says in verse twenty-two, *"And the keeper of the prison committed to Joseph's hand all the prisoners that were in the prison."* Even in prison, God gave Joseph favor. This reminds us that the Word of God says in Proverbs 22:1, *"A good name is rather to be chosen than great riches, and loving favour rather than silver and gold."*

In Genesis 39:23 we read, *"The keeper of the prison looked not to any thing that was under his hand; because the LORD was with him, and that which he did, the LORD made it to prosper."*

We want God to remove our problems. We want God to take away our prisons. However, God says, "I won't take away your problems or your prisons, but I'll go with you through your problems and be with you in your prisons."

The Bible tells us that a butler and a baker were in prison with Joseph. The butler lived and the baker died. The butler returned to Pharaoh's house. In Genesis 40:22-23 the Bible says, *"But he hanged the chief baker: as Joseph had interpreted to them. Yet did not the chief butler remember Joseph, but forgat him."*

We want God to work quickly, but God desires to work thoroughly.

If you study the life of Joseph and put events in chronological order, you will find that as a seventeen-year-old boy he was sold into slavery. For the next thirteen years, until he was thirty years of age, he was in Potiphar's house and in prison. The Lord worked thoroughly in Joseph's life. We want God to work quickly, but God desires to work thoroughly. Is God working thoroughly in your life?

The Lord delivered Joseph from prison. Pharaoh had a dream, and the butler remembered that Joseph could interpret dreams. Joseph was brought before Pharaoh and was enabled by God to interpret his dream. The Bible says in Genesis 41:38-41,

> *And Pharaoh said unto his servants, Can we find such a one as this is, a man in whom the Spirit of God is? And Pharaoh said unto Joseph, Forasmuch as God hath shewed thee all this, there is none so discreet and wise as thou art: thou shalt be over my house, and according unto thy word shall all my people be ruled: only in the throne will I be greater than thou. And Pharaoh said unto Joseph, See, I have set thee over all the land of Egypt.*

Although the butler had forgotten about Joseph for such a long time, it is evident that God never forgot Joseph. Beloved, no matter

what others have done to you, no matter what they have said about you, no matter what you have been through, God has not forsaken you.

SINNED AGAINST BY HIS BRETHREN

We find in God's Word that the Lord worked in Joseph's life even though his own brethren sinned against him. As we continue in this Bible story, we read in Genesis 42:1-4,

> *Now when Jacob saw that there was corn in Egypt, Jacob said unto his sons, Why do ye look one upon another? And he said, Behold, I have heard that there is corn in Egypt: get you down thither, and buy for us from thence; that we may live, and not die. And Joseph's ten brethren went down to buy corn in Egypt. But Benjamin, Joseph's brother, Jacob sent not with his brethren; for he said, Lest peradventure mischief befall him.*

The Lord worked to bring Joseph's brethren into his presence. The Bible says in Genesis 42:6-9,

> *And Joseph was the governor over the land, and he it was that sold to all the people of the land: and Joseph's brethren came, and bowed down themselves before him with their faces to the earth. And Joseph saw his brethren, and he knew them, but made himself strange unto them, and spake roughly unto them; and he said unto them, Whence come ye? And they said, From the land of Canaan to buy food. And Joseph knew his brethren, but they knew not him. And Joseph remembered the dreams which he dreamed of them, and said unto them, Ye are spies; to see the nakedness of the land ye are come.*

14

Do you know what Joseph really wanted to do? He wanted to rush to his brethren, embrace them, and smother them with kisses. However, they were not ready for this.

Do you know what our heavenly Joseph, the Lord Jesus, desires to do to us? He wants to rush to us, embrace us, and smother us with His kisses. But we must be prepared to receive Him. Just as they sinned against Joseph, we have sinned against our Lord Jesus and He must deal with us.

Let us notice how Joseph dealt with them. The Bible says in Genesis 42:15-16,

> *Hereby ye shall be proved: By the life of Pharaoh ye shall not go forth hence, except your youngest brother come hither. Send one of you, and let him fetch your brother, and ye shall be kept in prison, that your words may be proved, whether there be any truth in you: or else by the life of Pharaoh surely ye are spies.*

Remember when Joseph came to them, sent by his father, and his brothers said, "You're a spy, Joseph!" No doubt when Joseph said to them, "You're spies!" they thought that their great sin against their brother was catching up with them.

The Bible says in Genesis 42:20-23,

> *But bring your youngest brother unto me; so shall your words be verified, and ye shall not die. And they did so. And they said one to another, We are verily guilty concerning our brother, in that we saw the anguish of his soul, when he besought us, and we would not hear; therefore is this distress come upon us. And Reuben answered them, saying, Spake I not unto you, saying, Do not sin against the child; and ye*

would not hear? therefore, behold, also his blood is required. And they knew not that Joseph understood them; for he spake unto them by an interpreter.

The Word of God says in verse twenty-four that Joseph *"turned himself about from them, and wept."* Joseph was yearning; he was groaning. Inside, every emotion was tugging at him to embrace his brothers and reveal himself to them, but their hearts were not ready to receive him.

> *Oh, how much God desires to do for us! How tender and precious God desires to be to us, how He longs to bless us! But He must prepare our hearts to receive His blessing.*

Oh, how much God desires to do for us! How tender and precious God desires to be to us, how He longs to bless us! But He must prepare our hearts to receive His blessing.

The Bible says that Joseph kept Simeon, and the rest of his brothers traveled back to Canaan. They knew they were in trouble when they found their money in their bags. Things did not get better for them; instead, they were getting worse.

Do you know how we bring our burdens to the Lord? Do you know when we come to God and ask Him to help us? We come, not when the burden is light, but when the burden is so great we cannot bear it any longer.

The Bible says in Genesis 43:1, *"And the famine was sore in the land."* Joseph's brothers would have to go back to Egypt, but Joseph had asked them to bring Benjamin. The boys told Jacob, "He wants Benjamin."

Their father said, "No! He's all I have left. My tender wife, the one I loved so, gave me two sons and one is dead. You can't take Benjamin."

Finally, there was no other option. In Genesis 43:27-31 the Bible says,

> *And he asked them of their welfare, and said, Is your father well, the old man of whom ye spake? Is he yet alive? And they answered, Thy servant our father is in good health, he is yet alive. And they bowed down their heads, and made obeisance. And he lifted up his eyes, and saw his brother Benjamin, his mother's son, and said, Is this your younger brother, of whom ye spake unto me? And he said, God be gracious unto thee, my son. And Joseph made haste; for his bowels did yearn upon his brother: and he sought where to weep; and he entered into his chamber, and wept there. And he washed his face, and went out, and refrained himself, and said, Set on bread.*

Have you ever cried so much that you had to put cold water on your face to get rid of the expression that the tears and crying left? Joseph wanted so much to embrace his younger brother Benjamin, but he knew the timing was not right.

Finally, they started out on their journey back from Egypt, but Joseph's men overtook them and accused them of taking Joseph's silver cup. The brothers did not know that the cup had been planted in Benjamin's sack.

In Genesis 44:9-16 the Bible says,

> *With whomsoever of thy servants it be found, both let him die, and we also will be my lord's bondmen. And he said, Now also let it be according unto your words: he with whom it is found shall be my servant; and ye shall be blameless. Then they speedily took down every man his sack to the ground, and opened every man his sack. And he searched, and began at*

the eldest, and left at the youngest: and the cup was found in Benjamin's sack. Then they rent their clothes, and laded every man his ass, and returned to the city. And Judah and his brethren came to Joseph's house; for he was yet there: and they fell before him on the ground. And Joseph said unto them, What deed is this that ye have done? wot ye not that such a man as I can certainly divine? And Judah said, What shall we say unto my lord? what shall we speak? or how shall we clear ourselves? God hath found out the iniquity of thy servants: behold, we are my lord's servants, both we, and he also with whom the cup is found.

In other words, Judah said, "God has searched us and found us out! Our sin is inescapable!" Judah began to plead for Benjamin. He said to Joseph in Genesis 44:33-34,

> *Now therefore, I pray thee, let thy servant abide instead of the lad a bondman to my lord; and let the lad go up with his brethren. For how shall I go up to my father, and the lad be not with me? lest peradventure I see the evil that shall come on my father.*

At this point Judah died! I do not mean that he dropped over dead in Joseph's presence; but he died to self. In that moment, he said, "What happens to me and what you do with me no longer matters. There is something far more important and far greater than what happens to me." When Joseph saw that Judah had come to the end of himself, Joseph knew he could make himself known to his brethren.

When we come to the end of ourselves, then our sweet, precious Lord can make Himself truly known to us.

In Genesis 45:1-5 the Bible says,

> *Then Joseph could not refrain himself before all them that stood by him; and he cried, Cause every man to go out from me. And there stood no man with him, while Joseph made himself known unto his brethren. And he wept aloud: and the Egyptians and the house of Pharaoh heard. And Joseph said unto his brethren, I am Joseph; doth my father yet live? And his brethren could not answer him; for they were troubled at his presence. And Joseph said unto his brethren, Come near to me, I pray you. And they came near. And he said, I am Joseph your brother, whom ye sold into Egypt. Now therefore be not grieved, nor angry with yourselves, that ye sold me hither: for God did send me before you to preserve life.*

The story continues in Genesis 45:13-15,

> *And ye shall tell my father of all my glory in Egypt, and of all that ye have seen; and ye shall haste and bring down my father hither. And he fell upon his brother Benjamin's neck, and wept; and Benjamin wept upon his neck. Moreover he kissed all his brethren, and wept upon them: and after that his brethren talked with him.*

You may think, "I don't know how Joseph could forgive them. They sold him into slavery. They heard him cry out, 'Please don't do this to me! I cannot say goodbye to my father. Please don't sell me! Don't sin against me like this!'" But, Joseph forgave them completely. The Bible says Joseph kissed all of his brothers. These were kisses of forgiveness.

If we do not understand how Joseph could embrace and kiss his brothers who had sinned against him, may the Lord reveal to us something far greater. When we think of our Savior, we must realize that it was our sins, not His, that sent Him to the cross. The Bible says in Isaiah 53:5, *"But he was wounded for our transgressions, he was bruised for our iniquities: the chastisement of our peace was upon him; and with his stripes we are healed."*

Beloved, no matter what others have done to you, no matter what they have said about you, no matter what you have been through, God has not forsaken you.

Our sins drove the spikes and nails into His hands. We spat upon His face. We crowned Him with thorns. Yet our blessed Savior embraces us, hugs us, kisses us, brings us to Himself, and meets our every need. What a Savior! The Lord Jesus desires to do this and much more for us.

SENT BY GOD

Although Joseph was sold into slavery and sinned against by his brethren, he recognized that he was sent by God!

Joseph said, "Bring my father down." The tender scene when Jacob arrived is described for us in Genesis 46:29, *"And Joseph made ready his chariot, and went up to meet Israel his father, to Goshen, and presented himself unto him; and he fell on his neck, and wept on his neck a good while."*

Joseph showed his father the love he had stored up for all those years, the compassion, hugs, and kisses that he had wanted to give him all that time. God gave Joseph seventeen years with his father in Egypt, the same amount of time he had been at home before being sold by his brothers.

When Joseph grew old and was nearing death, he spoke to his brethren with great confidence in God. He looked back across his life and understood that God had sent him to Egypt in order to preserve the lives of many people, including his own father and family. He said to his brothers in Genesis 50:20, *"But as for you, ye thought evil against me; but God meant it unto good, to bring to pass, as it is this day, to save much people alive."*

> *When we think of our Savior, we must realize that it was our sins, not His, that sent Him to the cross.*

Joseph looked forward to the future and believed in the promise of God to His people. He said in Genesis 50:24, *"God will surely visit you, and bring you out of this land unto the land which he sware to Abraham, to Isaac, and to Jacob."* How can a man speak with such confidence? Because he came to know God and learned to trust Him.

Despite what is going on in this troubled world of ours, we can have communion with Christ and confidence in Him. He has taken the initiative. He has done His work. He is waiting for us to come to the place where He can bless us.

STRENGTH OUT OF SORROW

hen the Lord begins to work in someone's life, we never know exactly where that work will end. A boy comes walking across a field to find his brothers, and we follow him through the pages of Scripture until he becomes the most important part in one of the greatest movements of God in human history.

Very few people in the Word of God receive as much attention as Joseph. When the Lord places this much emphasis on someone or something, we should give earnest heed. Of course, God tells us so much about Joseph for a reason. We can learn many truths from his life. The sorrow he went through was used in strengthening him to be the man God desired for him to be.

The Bible says in Genesis 37:1-4,

> *And Jacob dwelt in the land wherein his father was a stranger, in the land of Canaan. These are the generations of Jacob. Joseph, being seventeen*

years old, was feeding the flock with his brethren; and the lad was with the sons of Bilhah, and with the sons of Zilpah, his father's wives: and Joseph brought unto his father their evil report. Now Israel loved Joseph more than all his children, because he was the son of his old age: and he made him a coat of many colours. And when his brethren saw that their father loved him more than all his brethren, they hated him, and could not speak peaceably unto him.

As we look at the life of Joseph, our story really begins seventeen years before the statements made in Genesis chapter thirty-seven. The favorite wife of Jacob, Rachel, had a little boy whose name was Joseph. Jacob was an old man by this time, and he loved this baby boy Joseph more than all his other children.

Most people who know only a little about the Bible know something about the life of Joseph. Joseph's brethren sold him into Egyptian bondage, and Joseph suffered greatly in Egypt. Then, he came to the place where he was as the Pharaoh of Egypt and actually was used of God to deliver the world from starvation because of what God had revealed to him.

When Joseph was a young man, God dealt with him in such a way to place within him what he would need to endure times of awful sorrow and great hours of temptation. God put something in his heart that he could hold to in the darkest hours of life. God built something into his character that made him into the giant of a man he became in Egypt to deliver the people of God. God prepared Joseph, not only by what He revealed to him through dreams, but also by what He allowed him to go through as a young man.

You may know about Moses the deliverer being called of God to go down into Egypt and deliver God's people from Egyptian bondage. But did you ever stop to think how God's people came to

Egypt, how they were preserved, and how a great nation was formed in the furnace of Egyptian suffering? This happened because God sent Joseph there. When the world was suffering from a terrible famine and nations could have starved to death, God revealed to Joseph how the world could be spared.

Consider carefully what Joseph went through as a young man and how this strengthened Joseph for what God had for his life. Strength came out of sorrow. Remember, Joseph was not just the child of any man; he was the son of Jacob. Jacob was not just any ordinary man; he was a man chosen of God for a special task.

In chapter twelve of the book of Genesis, God called Abraham out of Ur of the Chaldees. Through Abraham, God promised to build a great nation, and through that nation, to bless all people. Abraham was promised a land and a seed. Through Abraham, all the nations of the earth would be blessed.

Abraham had a son whose name was Isaac. Isaac had sons, Jacob and Esau. One of Jacob's sons was named Joseph. This means that Joseph's great-grandfather was Abraham. From all men, God chose Abraham and chose to build the nation of Israel out of the bosom of Abraham. Joseph's grandfather was Isaac, the son God promised to Abraham and Sarah. Joseph's father was Jacob, the one whose name was changed to *Israel* meaning, "a prince with God." Joseph had an amazing heritage. No doubt he realized all of this. His grandfather Isaac was still alive when Joseph was a boy.

> *If God is bringing things into our lives that are difficult to deal with because of our disobedience, the Lord will let us know the reason for our suffering.*

As a young man, Joseph had things take place in his life that shaped his character. Before he was ever dealt with severely by his brethren, God used sorrow to build him into the man He wanted him to be.

Why does God allow sorrowful things to happen to us? What is He doing in our lives by allowing such things? Dealing with sorrow is one of the most difficult things in all the world.

Most of the time, when someone suffers, people have the idea that he is suffering because of some terrible thing he has done. Perhaps one of the reactions you have about your own trouble is, "What did I do to deserve this?"

We find in the Bible that some suffering does come because of sin. The Word of God says in Galatians 6:7, *"For whatsoever a man soweth, that shall he also reap."*

> *Life is too wonderful to waste.*

If God is bringing things into our lives that are difficult to deal with because of our disobedience, the Lord will let us know the reason for our suffering. However, all sorrow is not because of our disobedience to God. Some of us are going to suffer simply because we are part of this human race and we are all dying people.

Some sorrow is allowed to come into our lives so that our hearts will be broken. We will be able to have compassion and love others who go through the same thing, testifying to them of God's grace.

Some sorrow is without explanation. I do not think there is any way to explain all suffering. Whatever the reason, the Lord wants to use suffering to bring us unto Himself.

You may think, "Why do I go through some of the things I go through? Why do I have the trouble I have with some of the people

I know? Why do I have problems? Why do I have sorrow?" Let me help you see that you can put your faith in the Lord in the hour of sorrow because God has a plan and purpose for you in it.

The Bible says in Genesis 35:7, *"And he built there an altar, and called the place Elbethel: because there God appeared unto him, when he fled from the face of his brother."* This verse commemorates the fact that Jacob feared Esau and was fleeing from Esau, yet God delivered him. During this time in Jacob's life, he met the Lord, and his name was changed.

Something tragic also took place about this time. The Word of God says in verse eight, *"But Deborah Rebekah's nurse died, and she was buried beneath Bethel under an oak."* Rebekah was the wife of Isaac. Isaac was the father of Jacob. Remember in Genesis chapter twenty-four when Abraham sent his servant to find a wife for Isaac. Abraham's servant came in contact with Rebekah, told her the story of Isaac, brought her back to Isaac, and Isaac took her as his wife.

When Rebekah followed the servant of Abraham back to Isaac, she brought her nurse with her. The name of Rebekah's nurse was Deborah. The Bible says that Deborah was of such importance that she stayed with Rebekah all the way from her father's house as she came to be the bride for Isaac.

In her old age, Deborah had become somewhat of a grandmother image to the sons of Jacob. Of course, she would have been a very dear person to Joseph. But Deborah died, and no doubt Joseph was greatly affected by her death.

Have you known anyone who was not really a blood relative, not really a mother, father, sister, or brother, but someone who was so dear to you, that when that person died, your heart was hurt deeply? Many people develop relationships like this in life. The Word of God says in Genesis chapter thirty-five that Deborah died.

Then the Bible says in Genesis 35:19, *"And Rachel died, and was buried in the way to Ephrath, which is Bethlehem."* Rachel was Jacob's wife and also Joseph's mother. Now Joseph's mother Rachel died. Rachel gave Jacob two children. Both of them were the children of his old age. Joseph was the first son she gave him, and while she was giving birth to Benjamin, she died and was buried in Bethlehem. If you travel today to Bethlehem, you will see the tomb of Rachel on the outskirts of town. Standing by that tomb on a number of occasions, I have thought of who stood on that piece of ground and what took place there. Joseph was certainly deeply affected by his mother's death.

In Genesis 35:27-29 the Bible says,

> *And Jacob came unto Isaac his father unto Mamre, unto the city of Arbah, which is Hebron, where Abraham and Isaac sojourned. And the days of Isaac were an hundred and fourscore years. And Isaac gave up the ghost, and died, and was gathered unto his people, being old and full of days: and his sons Esau and Jacob buried him.*

The Bible says that Jacob's father Isaac died. Isaac was Joseph's grandfather.

Many people have been extremely close to their grandparents and cherished the memories of time spent with them. How precious to sit with them, talk with them, enjoy their company, feel their love, and give your love to them.

In chapter thirty-five, the Bible says that Deborah died, Rachel died, and Isaac died. Do you wonder why a young man like Joseph suffered through the death of all those people so dear to him at one time? What was God doing in allowing such sorrow to come into young Joseph's life?

What you are going through may be something different than the death of a loved one. You may be suffering from heartache in your home. You may be going through something on your job. But all of us have some sorrow that God is allowing to come into our lives.

What strength can we gain for our lives out of sorrow? Why does God allow these things to come to us? Why does God allow our hearts to be broken? God wants to speak to us and deal with us. God wants our attention. The Lord opens our hearts through sorrow, trouble, and suffering. God opens our hearts to hear His Word and to strengthen us. My dear friend Dr. Lee Roberson said, "There is no greatness in life apart from trouble that is dealt with in the Spirit of Jesus Christ."

THE STRENGTH THAT CAME OUT OF SORROW CAUSED JOSEPH TO PLACE THE PROPER EMPHASIS ON LIFE

Allow me to point out some things that happened in Joseph's life because of this sorrow. Perhaps God will use them to speak to you. Because of the death of these loved ones, Joseph had occasion as a young man to place the proper emphasis on life and to consider the preciousness and value of life.

I doubt very seriously that you can attend anyone's funeral and not think about how precious it is to be alive. Think of the opportunities that are ours just to be alive. We complain about so many things when we should praise God that we are alive. We can breathe a breath of air and praise God for it. Life is too wonderful to waste. However, when someone near us dies, it causes us to stop and think long enough to place the proper emphasis on life.

I heard a popular man, who was involved in politics for many years of his life, make a statement in a news interview about his drug use. He had been rehabilitated from drug use. He said that only one third of the people who go into a rehabilitation program ever come out of it rehabilitated.

He went on to state, "As a servant of the United States in an elected office, when I got to the place in my life where I did not want to live because of what drugs were doing to me and I actually wanted to die because I thought it would be an easier way out, I knew I had problems severe enough to seek help." He wanted to die.

Are you excited about living? Are you grateful to God to have life? May God help you and me to place the proper emphasis on life.

As a young man, Joseph saw the preciousness of life and how wonderful and grand it was just to be alive. We find him in the pit where his brothers talked about killing him before one of his brothers delivered him. We follow his life down into the dark prison of Egypt when it looked as if everything was going wrong. We see all of this going on in Joseph's life, and we see that God had put something in him as a young man that helped him to carry on when things were tough. The Lord has a way of working to enable us to place the proper emphasis on life.

The Strength That Came out of Sorrow Caused Joseph to Place the Proper Emphasis on His Loved Ones

When someone we love dies, we have many emotions. Most of the time, we think of something we would have liked to have done for that loved one or with that loved one while he or she was alive.

When Deborah died, Joseph had opportunity to think about loved ones and what they meant to him. When Isaac died, he thought about his grandfather and how much he loved him. When his own mother died giving birth to his brother Benjamin, he had opportunity to think about how precious and wonderful his mother was to him.

Some people think very little of their mother or father. We have reached a time in our country when some parents despise their own children. We have developed a new term for this generation of children. They are called "throw-away children." Parents can do without them. How tragic! A survey done by Pennsylvania State University revealed that as many as one thousand children per week in America are abandoned by their parents. But God brings trouble, sorrow, and heartache into our lives at times to teach us how to love our loved ones more deeply and to show us how important our families truly are.

We should all learn from this Bible lesson to treat Mother as she should be treated, treat Dad as he should be treated, and treat sisters and brothers as they should be treated. God can speak to us through sorrow to place the proper emphasis on our loved ones. They will not be on this earth forever. If you ever intend to do anything to express the love you have for them, then you had better get busy and do it. You have no time to waste. Place the proper emphasis on your loved ones.

THE STRENGTH THAT CAME OUT OF SORROW CAUSED JOSEPH TO PLACE THE PROPER EMPHASIS ON THE LORD

Something else happened in the life of Joseph as a young boy that prepared him for the future and gave him strength out of sorrow. The death of these loved ones caused him to place the proper emphasis on the Lord. What does the Lord mean to you?

31

Most people give very little thought to dying and standing before God. More importantly, they give no thought to the fact that Christ died for them. We must tell people of the Savior.

Do you know why some people do not behave as they should toward the church? Because they do not love the Lord Jesus. If they loved the Lord Jesus, they would want to hear about Him. God allows things to come into our lives that cause us to place the proper emphasis on the Lord, and sometimes those things are sorrowful.

> *When Deborah died, Joseph had opportunity to think about life beyond death. He thought of people dying and standing before God.*

When Deborah died, Joseph had opportunity to think about life beyond death. He thought of people dying and standing before God. He thought about God. No doubt his father, whose life had been transformed by the power of God, told his son Joseph, "Put your faith and trust in the Lord and live for God with all your heart. No matter what comes to you, no matter what awful things befall you, keep your eyes on the Lord."

As we travel through the book of Genesis and arrive at the place where Joseph was down in the pit, sold into Egypt, and placed into prison, remember this young man had learned to keep his eyes on the Lord. God sustained him in the darkest of hours. The sorrow that the Lord allowed to come into his life opened his heart and allowed the Lord to speak to him about placing the priority on the Lord.

No wonder the Lord Jesus said in Matthew 11:28-29, *"Come unto me, all ye that labour and are heavy laden, and I will give you rest. Take my yoke upon you, and learn of me; for I am meek and lowly in heart: and ye shall find rest unto your souls."*

The Lord says to all those who labor and are heavy laden, who realize their need, whose hearts are burdened, who are facing sorrow, who feel the heavy weight upon them, *"Come unto me."* God does use sorrow, trouble, and heartache to help us see that we must trust Him.

The home where I grew up was not a Christian home. I believe that my parents loved me and I love them. But I do not know anything in my life that ever spoke to me anymore as a young man than the day I stood in the New Live Oak Cemetery in Selma, Alabama, and watched them lower the body of my father into a grave. I realized I would not hear his voice again. He was gone. I do not know of anything in my young life that did more to cause me to think about heaven and hell, the Lord, eternity, life, and loved ones anymore than that sorrow.

I certainly do not want someone to die in your family. But we can learn by the example of others that life is precious, family members are to be loved, and the Lord is to be given His proper place in our lives.

Chapter Three

THE LORD WAS WITH JOSEPH

 ooking back across my life, I can see clearly God's hand and His leading. He was with me all the time. He was directing me. He was closing doors that needed to be closed and opening doors that needed to be opened. He was guiding me, protecting me, and caring for me each step of the way to this present moment in my life.

No doubt there have been times in your life when you thought, "Where is the Lord?" I hope you realize that God is real and that He has been with you, guiding you, protecting you, sustaining you, and bringing you to this moment. He is *"the same yesterday, and to day, and for ever"* (Hebrews 13:8).

> *Joseph lost his coat, but he kept his character.*

As we view the life of Joseph, we read in Genesis 39:2, *"And the LORD was with Joseph, and he was a prosperous man; and he was in the house of his master the Egyptian."* Why was Joseph in Egypt?

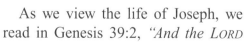

The Life of Joseph

God was in the process of building a great nation, the nation of Israel. Of all places, God did this work in the land of Egypt. The famous hymn by William Cowper describes it this way,

> God moves in a mysterious way
> His wonders to perform;
> He plants His footsteps in the sea,
> And rides upon the storm.
>
> Deep in unfathomable mines
> Of never-failing skill
> He treasures up His bright designs,
> And works His sovereign will.
>
> Ye fearful saints, fresh courage take,
> The clouds ye so much dread
> Are big with mercy, and shall break
> In blessings on your head.
>
> Judge not the Lord by feeble sense,
> But trust Him for His grace;
> Behind a frowning providence
> He hides a smiling face.
>
> His purposes will ripen fast,
> Unfolding every hour;
> The bud may have a bitter taste,
> But sweet will be the flower.
>
> Blind unbelief is sure to err,
> And scan His work in vain;
> God is His own interpreter,
> And He will make it plain.

There is a specific statement repeated over and over in chapter thirty-nine of the book of Genesis, *"The LORD was with Joseph."*

Verse three says, *"The LORD was with him,...the LORD made all that he did to prosper in his hand."*

Verse five says, *"The LORD blessed the Egyptian's house for Joseph's sake; and the blessing of the LORD was upon all that he had in the house, and in the field."*

The Word of God says again in verse twenty-one, *"But the LORD was with Joseph."*

You may think among the more than six billion people in the world today that you are all alone and God is a million miles away. If you are one of God's children, I hope you allow the Lord an opportunity to speak to you by His Spirit and come to realize that God is with you no matter where you may be. The Lord is with you, and He has brought you to this place because He desires to do a wonderful work in your life.

THE LORD WAS WITH JOSEPH IN THE HOUR OF LONELINESS

In the hour of Joseph's loneliness, the Lord was with him. Joseph was sent by his father to check on his brethren. Joseph loved them and he wanted to be with them. He wanted to find out how they were doing. He desired for them to love him.

When Joseph came to his brethren, they thought evil against him and sought to kill him. God stopped them through the influence of one of his brothers. After having thrown Joseph into a pit, they saw merchantmen traveling through their land on their way to Egypt. They thought, "We can sell Joseph to these people. We can get money for him, and they will take him into Egypt, and we will never see his face again." Of course, that is exactly what they did.

This account is given in Genesis 37:13-28. Read it carefully.

> *And Israel said unto Joseph, Do not thy brethren feed the flock in Shechem? come, and I will send thee unto them. And he said to him, Here am I. And he said to him, Go, I pray thee, see whether it be well with thy brethren, and well with the flocks; and bring me word again. So he sent him out of the vale of Hebron, and he came to Shechem. And a certain man found him, and, behold, he was wandering in the field: and the man asked him, saying, What seekest thou? And he said, I seek my brethren: tell me, I pray thee, where they feed their flocks. And the man said, They are departed hence; for I heard them say, Let us go to Dothan. And Joseph went after his brethren, and found them in Dothan. And when they saw him afar off, even before he came near unto them, they conspired against him to slay him. And they said one to another, Behold, this dreamer cometh. Come now therefore, and let us slay him, and cast him into some pit, and we will say, Some evil beast hath devoured him: and we shall see what will become of his dreams. And Reuben heard it, and he delivered him out of their hands; and said, Let us not kill him. And Reuben said unto them, Shed no blood, but cast him into this pit that is in the wilderness, and lay no hand upon him; that he might rid him out of their hands, to deliver him to his father again. And it came to pass, when Joseph was come unto his brethren, that they stript Joseph out of his coat, his coat of many colours that was on him; and they took him, and cast him into a pit: and the pit was empty, there was no water in it. And they*

sat down to eat bread: and they lifted up their eyes and looked, and, behold, a company of Ishmeelites came from Gilead with their camels bearing spicery and balm and myrrh, going to carry it down to Egypt. And Judah said unto his brethren, What profit is it if we slay our brother, and conceal his blood? Come, and let us sell him to the Ishmeelites, and let not our hand be upon him; for he is our brother and our flesh. And his brethren were content. Then there passed by Midianites merchantmen; and they drew and lifted up Joseph out of the pit, and sold Joseph to the Ishmeelites for twenty pieces of silver: and they brought Joseph into Egypt.

How in the world could God allow such a thing to happen? A seventeen-year-old boy left the safety of his father's side, went to check on his brothers, and they sold him into bondage. Words cannot describe how lonely Joseph must have been.

Think about your home. As I think of home, the fondest memories run through my mind. As Joseph was being carried off by the Ishmeelites down to Egypt, to a land where he had never been, I am sure he thought about his home and his father and he wondered how his brothers, if they ever loved him, could have done such a terrible thing to him. He was extremely lonely.

To Joseph, God was just as real down in Egypt in the house of Potiphar as He was back in Hebron in the house of Jacob.

Many people in our world are lonely. Some live with family members but are still lonely. They work at jobs with fifty or sixty people in the same area, yet they are lonely. Joseph was a lonely man carried down into Egypt away from his home and homeland, away from his family. The Bible says in the

hour of his loneliness, the Lord was with him. Just as the Lord was with Joseph, He has promised those who know Him, *"I will never leave thee, nor forsake thee"* (Hebrews 13:5).

I could not count the times people have said to me, "It was when I felt all alone that God became real to me and I turned to the Lord Jesus Christ." God brings us through times of loneliness and allows us to get to the place where it seems there is no one else in the world who really cares. Then we realize how much He cares, and we know that He is with us each step of the way.

THE LORD WAS WITH JOSEPH IN THE HOUR OF UNCERTAINTY

The Bible says in Proverbs 27:1, *"Boast not thyself of to morrow; for thou knowest not what a day may bring forth."* Joseph lived through a time of not knowing exactly what was going to happen to him. Try to imagine yourself in Joseph's place. His brothers sold him to merchantmen. He was traveling to Egypt with strangers who treated him as a slave. He did not know what was going to happen to him.

Life brings many hours of uncertainty. The Bible says the Lord was with Joseph. In Genesis 39:1 the Bible says, *"And Joseph was brought down to Egypt; and Potiphar, an officer of Pharaoh, captain of the guard, an Egyptian, bought him of the hands of the Ishmeelites, which had brought him down thither."*

Potiphar was an interesting character. In the land of Egypt, many men were in the military. Some were Egyptians, and some were from other countries. The Bible says this military man was an Egyptian. Not only was he a soldier and not only was he an Egyptian, he was a high-ranking officer in the Egyptian army. He was a captain. He was not just a captain in the Egyptian army, but a captain of the guard. Notice that the Bible says in verse one, *"And Joseph was brought down to Egypt; and Potiphar, an officer of Pharaoh, captain of the guard,..."*

There was a special group of Egyptian soldiers that were assigned to guard Pharaoh. They were very close to Pharaoh. Historians tell us that certain officers and certain soldiers were chosen for this specific assignment, and as many as one thousand soldiers had the sole responsibility of guarding the life of Pharaoh. The captain of this guard was a man by the name of Potiphar.

In God's providence, Joseph was sold as a slave to this man Potiphar. He was a soldier, a real man among men, a fighting man, a brave, courageous man. He was probably a rough kind of man, a man who was deliberate in his actions and in his speech, a man who was in charge of hundreds of other men.

Remember, Joseph had been at his father's side. He was the favorite son of twelve boys and was treated very kindly and tenderly by his loving father Jacob. Now Joseph was in Egypt in the household of a rough, tough man. God was working in the life of Joseph to get him ready for something great he must do.

In Joseph's hour of uncertainty, God was still there! Never was there an hour, a moment, or a day in the life of Joseph when the Lord was not with him. He is with us always!

Here was a little Hebrew slave who came all the way from the land of Canaan down to the land of Egypt. One of the mightiest of the soldiers took Joseph into his house. This little Hebrew boy went to Potiphar's house as a slave. But God was with him in the hour of uncertainty.

God never forsakes His own. We may have drifted from Him. We may have come to the place where we are no longer responsive to the things of the Lord as we once were, and we do not feel the nearness of the Spirit of God like we once did. But there is a God in heaven who never forsakes us. The Lord is with us in the hour of uncertainty.

There are moments when we do not know what to do, where to turn, or what decisions to make. Remember Joseph's life. In the hour of uncertainty, put your faith in the Lord Jesus Christ.

> *Not only was the Lord with Joseph, but also Potiphar was a witness to the fact that the Lord was with Joseph. When God has His hand on someone, others can see it.*

Are you a child of God? Have you asked God to forgive your sin and are you trusting in Christ and Christ alone as your Savior? Do you belong to the Lord? Have you sought to honor Him? God is with you in this hour of uncertainty.

The Bible says in Genesis 39:2-3, *"And the LORD was with Joseph, and he was a prosperous man; and he was in the house of his master the Egyptian. And his master saw that the LORD was with him, and that the LORD made all that he did to prosper in his hand."*

Not only was the Lord with Joseph, but also Potiphar was a witness to the fact that the Lord was with Joseph. When God has His hand on someone, others can see it. God blessed everything that Joseph did. When Joseph moved into Potiphar's house, he brought God with him, and God blessed the household of Potiphar for Joseph's sake.

The Bible says in verses four and five,

> *And Joseph found grace in his sight, and he served him: and he made him overseer over his house, and all that he had he put into his hand. And it came to pass from the time that he had made him overseer in his house, and over all that he had, that the LORD blessed the Egyptian's house for Joseph's sake; and*

the blessing of the LORD was upon all that he had in
the house, and in the field.

The slave had now become a master. In the household of Potiphar, of all the people working for the captain of the guard, Joseph was "as Potiphar" in the house. He was over everything. Think of how God worked in the hour of uncertainty.

THE LORD WAS WITH JOSEPH IN THE HOUR OF TEMPTATION

The Devil wants to bring together our weakness with evil temptation. This is what he sought to do in the life of Joseph. However, God was with Joseph in the hour of temptation. The Bible says in Genesis 39:7-9,

> *And it came to pass after these things, that his master's wife cast her eyes upon Joseph; and she said, Lie with me. But he refused, and said unto his master's wife, Behold, my master wotteth not what is with me in the house, and he hath committed all that he hath to my hand; there is none greater in this house than I; neither hath he kept back any thing from me but thee,...*

Joseph said to Potiphar's wife, "Your husband brought me in here and put everything in my hands. He has said to me that I have absolutely everything in this place except you." The Bible continues in verse nine, *"...because thou art his wife: how then can I do this great wickedness, and sin against God?"*

To Joseph, God was just as real down in Egypt in the house of Potiphar as He was back in Hebron in the house of Jacob. Joseph said, "I cannot sin against God and do this wickedness." If he had yielded to the temptation, he would have sinned against his own body. He would have sinned against Potiphar, the man who gave him responsibility. He would have sinned against Potiphar's wife. But most of all, he would have sinned against God. Joseph said, "I cannot do it." In the hour of temptation, the Lord was with him.

The slave had now become a master. In the household of Potiphar, of all the people working for the captain of the guard, Joseph was "as Potiphar" in the house.

The Bible says in I Corinthians 10:13, *"There hath no temptation taken you but such as is common to man: but God is faithful, who will not suffer you to be tempted above that ye are able; but will with the temptation also make a way to escape, that ye may be able to bear it."*

We have said so much about being able to bear temptation and escaping temptation. But the fact is, the Bible says the reason this is possible is that God is faithful.

In the hour of temptation, the Lord was with Joseph. Joseph gave this speech to Potiphar's wife, but that did not satisfy her. Genesis 39:10 says, *"And it came to pass, as she spake to Joseph day by day,..."* Relentlessly she went after him. *"...that he hearkened not unto her, to lie by her, or to be with her."* I think she may have changed her plea and said, "If you won't do this with me, why don't you just spend a little more time with me?"

Historians tell us that ancient Egyptian women had as much liberty as American women have today. In some countries, the custom was that women had to stay in a certain place and they were not to go from that place; but Egyptian women could do as they pleased in this particular matter.

The Bible says in verse eleven, *"And it came to pass about this time, that Joseph went into the house to do his business; and there was none of the men of the house there within."* Opportunity was at its worst for Joseph. No one was there to see anything he would do. He was all alone with this woman who had sought him time and time again. He was away from his homeland. He was in a land where women were free to do as they pleased. The Bible says he was in the house alone with her.

Verse twelve says, *"And she caught him by his garment, saying, Lie with me: and he left his garment in her hand, and fled, and got him out."* Joseph lost his coat, but he kept his character.

Verses thirteen through fifteen continue,

> *And it came to pass, when she saw that he had left his garment in her hand, and was fled forth, that she called unto the men of her house, and spake unto them, saying, See, he hath brought in an Hebrew unto us to mock us; he came in unto me to lie with me, and I cried with a loud voice: and it came to pass, when he heard that I lifted up my voice and cried, that he left his garment with me, and fled, and got him out.*

Potiphar's wife was a liar. But God was with Joseph in the hour of temptation. You may be in an awful mess, and things may be getting worse. You may be in the Devil's web, and it may seem as if you are caught and cannot get out. But if you know Jesus Christ as your Savior, God lives in you, and you have the power of the Holy Spirit available to overcome temptation and get the victory if you choose to do so. The Lord does not forsake us in our weak hours. God is with us in the hour of temptation.

THE LORD WAS WITH JOSEPH IN THE HOUR OF GREAT DISAPPOINTMENT

Have you ever been disappointed? Have you ever been disappointed with people? Of course you have. I have been disappointed with people in the Christian ministry. I have been disappointed with church members. I have been disappointed with friends. I have been disappointed with myself too many times to count.

Joseph was faithful to God. He lived for the Lord when no one was around to watch him. He was faithful when other men of weaker character would have yielded. What did he receive for his faithfulness? The Bible says in Genesis 39:16, *"And she laid up his garment by her, until his lord came home."* By the time Potiphar came home, his wife had devised a horrible scheme to destroy Joseph.

The Bible says in verses seventeen through nineteen,

> *And she spake unto him according to these words, saying, The Hebrew servant, which thou hast brought unto us, came in unto me to mock me: and it came to pass, as I lifted up my voice and cried, that he left his garment with me, and fled out. And it came to pass, when his master heard the words of his wife, which she spake unto him, saying, After this manner did thy servant to me; that his wrath was kindled.*

Remember what kind of man Potiphar was. He was captain of Pharaoh's guard. He was a man among men. He was a real soldier. When he heard this news from his wife, he was angry. His wrath was kindled. He felt like a wild bear, and he went after Joseph. The Bible says in verse twenty, *"And Joseph's master took him, and put him into the prison, a place where the king's prisoners were bound: and he was there in the prison."*

Notice carefully what God says in His Word in verses twenty-one through twenty-three,

> But the LORD was with Joseph, and shewed him mercy, and gave him favour in the sight of the keeper of the prison. And the keeper of the prison committed to Joseph's hand all the prisoners that were in the prison; and whatsoever they did there, he was the doer of it. The keeper of the prison looked not to any thing that was under his hand; because the LORD was with him, and that which he did, the LORD made it to prosper.

God is with us in the hour of great disappointment. Can you imagine how disappointed Joseph was when this woman lied about him and her husband believed her lies and cast Joseph into prison?

Remember, there is no disappointment in Jesus Christ. In the hour of disappointment, the Lord is with you. In the hour of loneliness, in the hour of temptation, in the hour of uncertainty, in the hour of awful disappointment, all that has sustained me is to know the Lord is with me.

Friend, the Lord is with us to sustain us. It did not take long for Joseph to find out that the Lord was with him in jail. God was with Joseph in prison just as God was with him at Hebron. God was with Joseph as he traveled to Egypt, and God was in Potiphar's house. When Joseph got to prison, God was there waiting for him. God's Word says, *"The LORD was with Joseph."*

Chapter Four

WHEN GOD WORKS ON THE OTHER END

he Lord is at work in the lives of people. We often have an easier time believing that God can work in us than believing He can work in the lives of those for whom we are concerned. We need to realize that God works on both ends. While Joseph was in prison, his God was working on his behalf in the palace of Pharaoh.

The Bible says in Genesis 41:1-14,

And it came to pass at the end of two full years, that Pharaoh dreamed: and, behold, he stood by the river. And, behold, there came up out of the river seven well favoured kine and fatfleshed; and they fed in a meadow. And, behold, seven other kine came up after them out of the river, ill favoured and leanfleshed; and stood by the other kine upon the brink of the river. And the ill favoured and leanfleshed kine did eat up the seven well favoured and fat kine. So Pharaoh awoke.

And he slept and dreamed the second time: and, behold, seven ears of corn came up upon one stalk, rank and good. And, behold, seven thin ears and blasted with the east wind sprung up after them. And the seven thin ears devoured the seven rank and full ears. And Pharaoh awoke, and, behold, it was a dream. And it came to pass in the morning that his spirit was troubled; and he sent and called for all the magicians of Egypt, and all the wise men thereof: and Pharaoh told them his dream; but there was none that could interpret them unto Pharaoh. Then spake the chief butler unto Pharaoh, saying, I do remember my faults this day: Pharaoh was wroth with his servants, and put me in ward in the captain of the guard's house, both me and the chief baker: and we dreamed a dream in one night, I and he; we dreamed each man according to the interpretation of his dream. And there was there with us a young man, an Hebrew, servant to the captain of the guard; and we told him, and he interpreted to us our dreams; to each man according to his dream he did interpret. And it came to pass, as he interpreted to us, so it was; me he restored unto mine office, and him he hanged. Then Pharaoh sent and called Joseph, and they brought him hastily out of the dungeon: and he shaved himself, and changed his raiment, and came in unto Pharaoh.

Think about what has happened in the life of Joseph. Notice what the Bible says in verse one, *"And it came to pass at the end of two full years, that Pharaoh dreamed: and, behold, he stood by the river."* Two full years had gone by since Joseph had been falsely accused and placed in the king's prison for a crime he did not commit. In the house of Potiphar, the captain of the guard, Potiphar's wife had attempted to seduce Joseph. Joseph ran from her, leaving his coat but keeping his character.

When Potiphar came home, his wife said to him, "I want you to see what this Hebrew has done. He has disgraced our household. He has tried to do these awful things to me."

Potiphar's anger was kindled against Joseph, and he cast him into prison. When Joseph was in prison, God gave him favor in the eyes of the prison keeper, and Joseph was given a responsibility over the other prisoners in the jail.

While Joseph was there, two of Pharaoh's servants, his baker and his butler, were cast into prison with Joseph. While they were there, they had dreams and they were troubled because of those dreams. They went to Joseph, and he interpreted their dreams. Just as Joseph had said, the butler was restored to the service of Pharaoh, the king of Egypt, and the baker was put to death.

Millions have come to the Lord because someone on this end prayed and God worked on the other end to bring them to Christ.

Before the butler left prison, he made a promise to Joseph. He promised that he would remember Joseph when he got out of prison and that he would put in a good word to Pharaoh for Joseph's sake. Not long after he made this promise, the butler was delivered and restored to his position. Joseph thought that he would soon hear a rattling of the bars in the prison and someone would come for him because of the butler's message to Pharaoh.

The days passed and no word came. Weeks passed by and no word came. Two full years had passed and Joseph began to think that nothing was going to happen, at least not like the butler said it would happen. Of course, Joseph's faith was not in the butler but in God.

I imagine that during this time of loneliness, Joseph comforted himself with thoughts of home. He had been removed from the land of his upbringing and brought down into Egypt. He had been placed in a prison only to be forgotten by one who told him he would faithfully remember him.

Honor the Lord and He will honor you.

Joseph talked to God, and God worked in the life of Joseph. As Joseph prayed, he knew that God was real to him. However, I want to emphasize that while God worked in the life of Joseph, He also worked on the other end.

All of us have difficulties with which to deal. Our difficulties may be in the home. Our difficulties may be on the job. Our difficulties may be with people with whom we have tried to work and seemingly failed. Whatever the circumstances may be, all of us face some difficulty in our lives. But God is at work on the other end. God is working in the lives of people that we have to deal with, people whose lives touch our lives day by day. God is working on the other end.

GOD DESERVES TO BE HONORED

In this story we learn that God deserves to be honored. In I Samuel chapter two the Lord was speaking, warning Eli the priest. The Word of God says in verse thirty, *"Wherefore the LORD God of Israel saith, I said indeed that thy house, and the house of thy father, should walk before me for ever: but now the LORD saith, Be it far from me; for them that honour me I will honour, and they that despise me shall be lightly esteemed."*

Notice what the Bible says, *"Them that honour me I will honour."* Honor the Lord and He will honor you.

Do you believe there is a real God in heaven who sees us and knows all about us? Do you believe that, no matter what we are saying or what people around us are doing, God really sees our hearts and knows what is going on inside of us? The Word of God promises that if we honor Him, He will honor us.

Let us go back to our story of Joseph in the book of Genesis. Remember that Joseph was in prison. No one saw him but a few men who were locked in jail with him. Yet, he was true to the Lord.

Back in Potiphar's house, Joseph had been alone in the house with Potiphar's wife. She told him, "No one is here. I've sent everyone out. Absolutely no eye beholds what is going on in this house. All the servants are gone."

But God was real to Joseph, and Joseph honored God and said, "I will not sin against God." Now Joseph was in jail. He continued to do what was right. Everything seemed to have gone wrong, but God was not finished. Joseph realized that the Lord deserves our honor.

When we talk about God and all that He is, we realize that He certainly deserves to be honored. We know that He is eternal, almighty, omnipotent, and omniscient. God's Word teaches that He is omnipresent. This means that God is not only here with us, proving Himself through what He does, but also that He is everywhere at the same time. If this is true of our Lord, and if God can work here today, on our end, God can also work on the other end.

I have spent most of my life trying to get things from God before I was ready to receive them or before God was ready to give them to me.

Think of one person who has a need, someone you know and love who needs the Lord at this moment. That person needs God's care and keeping in his life. I want you to know that God can work on that end of the line just as readily as He can work in your heart at this moment. You may ask, "How do you know that?" We find this to be true in the Word of God.

> While Joseph was in prison his God was working on his behalf in the palace of Pharaoh.

Joseph was in jail. Joseph was trusting God. Joseph was praying to the Lord and honoring the Lord. When Potiphar's wife tempted Joseph, Joseph was the one who acknowledged the Lord and said that he would not sin against God.

When the butler and baker had dreams, Joseph was the one who said to them that God would give the interpretation. But God was also working on the other end in the heart of Pharaoh and in the heart of the butler.

We need to be reminded again and again about what our God is able to do. If we will honor Him, He will honor us. My confidence is not in what I can do. My confidence is not in what I am able to say. My confidence is not in what I might be able to share with others from the Word of God. My confidence is in the quiet place, in the secret place of my life, where I have chosen to honor God and I believe that God will keep His Word.

GOD SPEAKS TO MEN

As we look at this story, we realize also that God speaks to men. The Bible says in Hebrews 1:1-3,

> *God, who at sundry times and in divers manners spake in time past unto the fathers by the prophets, hath in these last days spoken unto us by his Son, whom he hath appointed heir of all things, by whom also he made the worlds; who being the brightness of*

54

his glory, and the express image of his person, and upholding all things by the word of his power, when he had by himself purged our sins, sat down on the right hand of the Majesty on high.

God spoke through the prophets, and God also speaks today. I am thankful that we do not have to bow down to a dumb idol. We do not have a god of wood or stone. We do not pray to a picture hanging on the wall or an image displayed somewhere. We have a true and living God who speaks to people. The Bible declares of our God in Isaiah 45:18-23,

> *For thus saith the LORD that created the heavens; God himself that formed the earth and made it; he hath established it, he created it not in vain, he formed it to be inhabited: I am the LORD; and there is none else. I have not spoken in secret, in a dark place of the earth: I said not unto the seed of Jacob, Seek ye me in vain: I the LORD speak righteousness, I declare things that are right. Assemble yourselves and come; draw near together, ye that are escaped of the nations: they have no knowledge that set up the wood of their graven image, and pray unto a god that cannot save. Tell ye, and bring them near; yea, let them take counsel together: who hath declared this from ancient time? who hath told it from that time? have not I the LORD? and there is no God else beside me; a just God and a Saviour; there is none beside me. Look unto me, and be ye saved, all the ends of the earth: for I am God, and there is none else. I have sworn by myself, the word is gone out of my mouth in righteousness, and shall not return, That unto me every knee shall bow, every tongue shall swear.*

Have you heard from God today? Has God said anything to you? Has God dealt with you? I would hate to imagine that God works only in me. If God does not work on the other end, then my labor is in vain. God does work on the other end.

I believe you can get on your knees and pray to God for your mother today, and just as surely as you know you are talking to God on this end, God can speak to your mother on the other end. You can pray for your father today, and just as surely as you know God is working in your heart on this end, God will work in the heart of your father on the other end. God's work on the other end is just as certain as God's work on this end.

Millions have come to the Lord because someone on this end prayed and God worked on the other end to bring them to Christ. This is the way the Lord works. This is the way God moves. God speaks to people.

In Psalm 85:8 the Bible says, *"I will hear what God the Lord will speak: for he will speak peace unto his people, and to his saints: but let them not turn again to folly."* God will speak to us. If you have read Genesis chapter forty-one, you know that through a dream God stirred Pharaoh and also prodded the memory of the butler. God spoke to those men. God dealt with them.

God Speaks Through His Word

God speaks to us today through His Word, the Bible, the eternal Word of God. Many times I have gone to God in a low hour of my life, and God used a Bible verse like a spiritual pulley to hold me up, lift me up, and do something for me nothing else could do. God speaks to us through His Word. Read a portion of His Word each day and meditate upon it.

GOD SPEAKS THROUGH HIS SPIRIT

God speaks to us by His Spirit. The Spirit of God indwells every believer. How many times in a place of surrender and submission to the Lord have you said, "God, guide me and direct me"? Have you sensed in your heart the Lord leading in a certain direction, confirming in your thinking the way to go, the way to respond? By His Spirit, He speaks to us. The Bible says in Isaiah 30:21, *"And thine ears shall hear a word behind thee, saying, This is the way, walk ye in it, when ye turn to the right hand, and when ye turn to the left."*

GOD SPEAKS THROUGH OTHER CHRISTIANS

God speaks to us through other Christians. God has spoken to me so many times through other people as they have given to me *"a word fitly spoken...like apples of gold in pictures of silver"* (Proverbs 25:11). Perhaps they did not know at the time that God was speaking through them, but as they said things, God used them to speak to me.

GOD SPEAKS THROUGH CIRCUMSTANCES

God speaks to us through circumstances. Most of us think we are living under our circumstances. We should live on top of them and walk through them victoriously. Sometimes we get the idea we are the only people in the world having a hard time. The fact is, God allows the circumstances, and through the circumstances He speaks to us. So often our disappointments are His appointments.

Pharaoh had a dream; something circumstantial took place in his life. He called for his magicians and wise men to come, and they were confounded. This was a very simple dream, and when Joseph interpreted it, it seemed like such a simple matter. But they stumbled over it. The wisdom of this world is confounded by *"the simplicity that is in Christ"* (II Corinthians 11:3).

After God spoke to Pharaoh and worked in the memory of Pharaoh's butler, they called for Joseph. The Bible says Joseph shaved himself. Historians tell us that the Egyptians were clean-shaven people. The Hebrews were people who grew beards. Evidently, Joseph had grown a beard in prison, so he shaved himself, and he was brought into the court of royalty.

Can you imagine this boy sold into bondage to Ishmeelite merchantmen, carried down to Egypt, cast into prison, loosed from prison, walking into the royal court of Pharaoh? I can only imagine what it must have been like that day when Pharaoh, the most powerful man in Egypt, sat on his throne and Joseph, this young Hebrew, was brought before him straight from prison. God was about to deliver Joseph from prison and make a prince out of him. Why? I remind you that it was because he honored God and God honored him.

I do not think any young man or young woman has ever lived without a dream, thinking about what it would be like to do certain things. Everyone understands what it is like to think, to pray, and to believe and then to have times in life when it seems as if all your dreams have died and everything is gone. But God was about to bring something wonderful to pass in the life of Joseph.

GOD DOES WHAT IS RIGHT AT THE RIGHT TIME

We learn also from this story that God does what is right at the right time. Imagine if the butler had gone out and said, "Pharaoh, I just got out of jail this morning, and I want to tell you there is a Hebrew boy down there that is wiser than anyone I've ever met. He can tell you what dreams mean. I'd like for you to get him a job somewhere."

Imagine if Pharaoh said, "Well, we gave him a try in Potiphar's house." By the way, they changed Joseph's name and though we cannot be absolutely sure, some authors believe the name Pharaoh gave him meant, "a man who has been cleared from adultery." It is amazing how God takes care of everything.

What if the butler had come out of prison two years earlier and said, "I wish you would do something for him." And Pharaoh said, "I think I can find him a job somewhere." Maybe he would have given him a responsibility of esteem somewhere. But no, it did not happen that way. The timing was not right.

God does what is right, when it is right to do it. When Pharaoh had a burden and his heart was troubled, then God worked on the memory of the butler to tell Pharaoh about Joseph. The Word of God tells us the story. As Pharaoh repeated his dream in Genesis 41:17-18, the Bible says, *"And Pharaoh said unto Joseph, In my dream, behold, I stood upon the bank of the river: and, behold, there came up out of the river seven kine, fatfleshed and well favoured; and they fed in a meadow."*

Joseph said, "Pharaoh, the interpretation belongs to God, and this is what your dream means. It means there are going to be seven years of plenty and then seven years of famine."

Joseph not only told Pharaoh what was wrong, but he also said, "Here's what you need to do. You need to find someone who can administrate this and gather all the food you can gather in the seven years of plenty. Put it all in the cities and take care of it and administrate it during the years of famine." Joseph was not trying to

> *I believe you can get on your knees and pray to God for your mother today, and just as surely as you know you are talking to God on this end, God can speak to your mother on the other end.*

get the job, he was simply trying to be faithful to God and tell Pharaoh what needed to be done.

Pharaoh looked around at all his wise men and thought, "There's not one of these men who can handle this kind of job. Since you're the one that God spoke to, I'm going to make you second in command in Egypt."

As I came to this passage in the Bible, I thought, "It is amazing what God can do in a moment." With a snap of the finger, Joseph was over even Potiphar and Potiphar's wife. Pharaoh said, "I ride in the main chariot, Joseph, but you will ride in the second chariot that runs behind me. We're going to ride all over Egypt and tell everyone who you are. We're going to let all of Egypt know that you are as Pharaoh in the land of Egypt."

Just minutes before, Joseph came hastily from the jail which was evidently connected some way close to the palace. Think what God can do when He is ready to do it. Reading a story like this should increase your faith and make you love the Lord even more.

When I was a boy, my mother would cook wonderful meals for us. One of our favorite things she prepared was chocolate cake. She would work very diligently making it from scratch. She placed it in the pan and put it in the oven. We knew when it came out, it was going to be very good.

She would bring it out of the oven and reach for a toothpick to check it. If she pulled the toothpick out of the cake, and it had dough sticking to it, the cake was not done. We hoped that there would be nothing on that toothpick.

I remember times when she would stick the toothpick down into the cake and there would still be a little dough on it. She would say, "I have to put it back in." I wanted it so badly I could have grabbed it and eaten it hot with the dough running on the inside. But she knew when it would be ready. When it was ready, she got it out and served it to us. It was delicious, but we had to wait until it was ready.

I have spent most of my life trying to get things from God before I was ready to receive them or before God was ready to give them to me. We need to be renewed in our faith that God will always do what is right, and He will do it when it is right to do it. He knows when the timing is right. The Bible actually teaches that God waits for the right moment to be gracious to us. Read carefully Isaiah 30:18, *"And therefore will the LORD wait, that he may be gracious unto you, and therefore will he be exalted, that he may have mercy upon you: for the LORD is a God of judgment: blessed are all they that wait for him."*

Think what God can do when He is ready to do it.

The time was perfect and the need was great in the land of Egypt. God had diligently prepared a man to meet the need, and God raised him up from prison and made him as Pharaoh in Egypt. All this was accomplished because God works on the other end.

Chapter
Five

THE BLESSINGS OF GOD DURING THE DAYS OF AFFLICTION

 oseph is no longer a teenager when we come to chapter forty-one in the book of Genesis. He was recognized by Pharaoh in Egypt as a man who knew God. He interpreted Pharaoh's dream, and the confidence of the king of Egypt was placed in Joseph. Joseph was exalted to a position next to Pharaoh in Egypt.

The Bible says in Genesis 41:41-57,

> *And Pharaoh said unto Joseph, See, I have set thee over all the land of Egypt. And Pharaoh took off his ring from his hand, and put it upon Joseph's hand, and arrayed him in vestures of fine linen, and put a gold chain about his neck; and he made him to ride in the second chariot which he had; and they cried before him, Bow the knee: and he made him ruler over all the land of Egypt. And Pharaoh said unto Joseph, I am Pharaoh, and without thee shall no man lift up his hand or foot*

63

in all the land of Egypt. And Pharaoh called Joseph's name Zaphnathpaaneah; and he gave him to wife Asenath the daughter of Potipherah priest of On. And Joseph went out over all the land of Egypt. And Joseph was thirty years old when he stood before Pharaoh king of Egypt. And Joseph went out from the presence of Pharaoh, and went throughout all the land of Egypt. And in the seven plenteous years the earth brought forth by handfuls. And he gathered up all the food of the seven years, which were in the land of Egypt, and laid up the food in the cities: the food of the field, which was round about every city, laid he up in the same. And Joseph gathered corn as the sand of the sea, very much, until he left numbering; for it was without number. And unto Joseph were born two sons before the years of famine came, which Asenath the daughter of Potipherah priest of On bare unto him. And Joseph called the name of the firstborn Manasseh: For God, said he, hath made me forget all my toil, and all my father's house. And the name of the second called he Ephraim: For God hath caused me to be fruitful in the land of my affliction. And the seven years of plenteousness, that was in the land of Egypt, were ended. And the seven years of dearth began to come, according as Joseph had said: and the dearth was in all lands; but in all the land of Egypt there was bread. And when all the land of Egypt was famished, the people cried to Pharaoh for bread: and Pharaoh said unto all the Egyptians, Go unto Joseph; what he saith to you, do. And the famine was over all the face of the earth: And Joseph opened all the storehouses, and sold unto the Egyptians; and the famine waxed sore in the land of Egypt. And all

countries came into Egypt to Joseph for to buy corn; because that the famine was so sore in all lands.

Notice in verse fifty-one the word *"forget,"* and in verse fifty-two the word *"fruitful."* Joseph had been given a very special position with great authority over all the land of Egypt. God revealed to Joseph that there would be seven years of plenty when the crops would be bountiful. After the seven fruitful years, there would be seven years of famine when there would be nothing.

The Word of God reveals to us that this famine was not only in Egypt but also in other lands as well. Egypt literally became the breadbasket for the world. People from other countries heard that there was food in Egypt, and they came in the midst of the awful famine to Egypt and received from Joseph the food they needed to live.

Before Joseph ever came to this place of distinction, many things happened in his life. Years had passed. As a seventeen-year-old boy, he had been taken by his brothers and sold to the Ishmeelite merchantmen traveling down to Egypt.

> *Joseph made up his mind in Egypt, not in Canaan, to find contentment in God's will.*

He had been a slave in Egypt. He came into Potiphar's house. He was falsely accused and sent to prison. After his years in prison, he came out and interpreted Pharaoh's dream. He was given an exalted position in Egypt.

After all this, Joseph took Asenath to be his wife. The Bible says her father was the priest of On. Joseph and his wife had two children. The names of these children specifically reflect what had been going on in the life of Joseph.

The Bible says in Genesis 41:50-52,

> *And unto Joseph were born two sons before the years of famine came, which Asenath the daughter of Potipherah priest of On bare unto him. And Joseph called the name of the firstborn Manasseh: For God, said he, hath made me forget all my toil, and all my father's house. And the name of the second called he Ephraim: For God hath caused me to be fruitful in the land of my affliction.*

Joseph named his first son *"Manasseh"* declaring, "This is what I have forgotten." He named his second son *"Ephraim"* declaring, "This is what God has blessed me with." Their names tell the story of what was gone and what was given.

Much of our lives are spent in disappointment if we can only see the affliction and we fail to see the blessings of God. We identify what is gone and often fail to see what is given. Much of our time is spent dealing with our troubles instead of recognizing our blessings.

God gives blessings in the days of affliction. Joseph was in a strange land. He was not an Egyptian; he was a Hebrew. This was not his home. His father's name was Jacob. Joseph loved his father. He was beloved of his father, rejected by his brethren, sold for silver, and received by a Gentile bride.

This sounds so very familiar as we think of our Lord Jesus Christ who *"came unto his own, and his own received him not"* (John 1:11). He was sold for thirty pieces of silver and was rejected by the Jews. He also received a Gentile. Of course, some day He will reveal Himself to His brethren, the Jews, just as Joseph revealed himself to his brethren.

Joseph was in a place of affliction. He was in a strange place, a place he would never truly call home. After years of living in Egypt,

Joseph would say to his brethren, "When I die, get my bones out of here." And they did carry his bones out of Egypt and took them back to the land of his birth to bury them.

If we are going to live victoriously, we must by faith see the Lord in the midst of our situation. We must see the blessings of God during the days of affliction. We must recognize that in the midst of the clouds, the sun is still shining.

I think it is so wonderful that God reveals to us this lesson in Joseph's sons. He said that one of them represented all he had forgotten and the other represented fruitfulness. One represented what was gone, the other what was given.

OUR FORGETTING

In Genesis 41:51 the Bible says, *"And Joseph called the name of the firstborn Manasseh: For God, said he, hath made me forget all my toil, and all my father's house."*

This does not mean that Joseph forgot his father. Joseph did not forget that his brothers existed. I do not believe Joseph forgot the place where he grew up as a boy and all the fond memories he cherished from his boyhood days. To say that he "forgot" means that Joseph was able to get over his hurt and get on with his life. He was able to forget. He was able to get over the heartache and get on with living. He was able to go beyond his afflictions and live a victorious life.

Did it ever dawn on you that there is not one perfect person alive? There is not one perfect person or one perfect place on this earth. Did you ever think about the fact that you are not perfect and no one you live with is perfect? The Bible says this about sin, *"For all have sinned, and come short of the glory of God"* (Romans 3:23).

I am amused when people come to me wanting to get married and they think they have found the first perfect mate. The fellow really

believes that he has found the perfect wife, and she believes she has found the perfect husband. They are not together long before they realize that we are all imperfect.

> *There is a time to stop crying and start living again. This is accomplished by God's grace.*

Many people live in the past. They will not forgive. It is not what has happened to them that hurts most; it is their unwillingness to get over what has happened. They will not get over things and get on with life. Because of this, they cannot have God's blessings in all their troubles. They cannot see God's goodness in their time of affliction.

In Philippians 3:10-14 the Bible says,

> *That I may know him, and the power of his resurrection, and the fellowship of his sufferings, being made conformable unto his death; if by any means I might attain unto the resurrection of the dead. Not as though I had already attained, either were already perfect: but I follow after, if that I may apprehend that for which also I am apprehended of Christ Jesus. Brethren, I count not myself to have apprehended: but this one thing I do, forgetting those things which are behind, and reaching forth unto those things which are before, I press toward the mark for the prize of the high calling of God in Christ Jesus.*

Did Paul mean that he had forgotten everything about the stoning of Stephen? Did he mean that he had forgotten about being stoned and left for dead in Lystra? What did he mean? He simply meant that he had been able by the grace of God to get to the place in his life where he could get over the past and get on with his life. He could leave the past.

I wonder how many people would say, "My big issue in life is that I keep living in the past, bringing up the past with those I love. I just have the hardest time getting over it and getting on with my life." You are miserable and you are making others miserable who know you and love you because you will not get over it.

Imagine that Joseph had said, "You don't realize what I've gone through. You don't understand. I had everything going for me. I lived in a nearly perfect home. My dad was Jacob, the son of Isaac and grandson of Abraham. You don't know who I am. You don't know where I lived. You don't understand this. I had everything I wanted. My brothers sold me to Ishmeelite merchantmen. They took me from my home and brought me down to Egypt. Do you understand what I am saying to you? I've had it rough. I've had it hard. I went into a man's house by the name of Potiphar. I tried to live for God and be true to God and Potiphar's wife lied about me. They cast me into prison. In prison I tried to do what was right. I made friends with people. A man told me his dream, and I interpreted it. That fellow promised me when he got out that he would remember me. He forgot me."

Suppose Joseph had gone on like that. This is the way many people live. They live in the past. May God help us to forget those things which are behind.

Our God is not confined to geographical locations.

This world is not perfect. The Bible says this world is getting worse and worse. But in the midst of this, we must not fail to see the goodness of God in the days of affliction. God help us to see His blessings during the days of our heartache.

OUR FRUITFULNESS

I am glad God gave Joseph two boys, and I am glad Joseph named them what he did, because it shows us not only what is gone but also what is given. Genesis 41:51 says, *"And Joseph called the name of the firstborn Manasseh: For God, said he, hath made me forget all my toil, and all my father's house."* Many people could live a life of blessing but never will if they do not choose to get over the past and get on with their lives. There is a time to stop crying and start living again. This is accomplished by God's grace. The Bible continues in verse fifty-two, *"And the name of the second called he Ephraim: For God hath caused me to be fruitful in the land of my affliction."* Joseph said, "God has been good to me. In spite of all that has gone wrong, I have seen God's blessing."

> The *"prime of life"* is anytime in life when we are in the center of God's will.

Joseph made up his mind in Egypt, not in Canaan, to find contentment in God's will. God had allowed it. God had him there for a purpose. Joseph declared that by God's grace he was going to see God's blessings in the land of affliction. We find the peace of God only as we surrender to the will of God.

I do not know how long I am going to live on this earth. I do not know how quickly I will be finished. I do not know how many days, months, or years I have left. As we yield our lives to the Lord Jesus Christ, we can make the most of the life we have left.

When Joseph was taken from the land of his birth, the land of his father, he had no family. But look what God did. God gave him a wife and God gave him sons. God gave him a family. The "prime of life" is anytime in life when we are in the center of God's will.

When Joseph was taken down to Egypt, he had no position. He had been the favorite among his brothers. But look what God did for him. In that strange land, God made him as Pharaoh in Egypt.

Joseph thought, "God has given me so much." And he named his son Ephraim because God had blessed him.

OUR FAITHFUL LORD

Our God is not confined to geographical locations. God was real to Joseph when Joseph was down in Hebron with his father. But God was just as real to Joseph when he was in Potiphar's prison. God is real. Our Lord is faithful. God will bless and use you. If you want to see the blessings of God in the days of affliction, you can. The Bible says of our God, *"He abideth faithful"* (II Timothy 2:13).

I imagine since mamas and daddies have been having boys and girls, there have been certain things that all mamas and daddies have done. When I was just a boy growing up, my mother would take me into her arms when I was hurt. If I had fallen on the sidewalk or perhaps I had a little scratch on my finger, my mother would say to me like your mother has said to you, and like we say to our children when they are very young, "Where does it hurt?" I would show her where it hurt and she would say, "Let me kiss it where it hurts." She would kiss it right where it was hurting.

If we are going to live victoriously, we must by faith see the Lord in the midst of our situation.

Then, she would say to me, "Doesn't that feel better?"

I would reply, "Yes, that helped to have you kiss it where it hurts."

God created a perfect world. God created two people and He put them in it. Sin came and God's perfect world was cursed by sin.

We still live in that sin-cursed world, and we are sinful people. But I want you to know, since the dawning of creation in the Garden of Eden, our Lord has looked on mankind and said, "I know you are hurting. I know in these days and places of affliction, there are things that go wrong. But I will be faithful to you and I will kiss it where it hurts and help you through."

Their names tell the story of what was gone and what was given.

When I was just a teenage boy, I gave my life to the Lord Jesus Christ. I know He saved me. I received Him as my Savior. I confessed to Him that I was a sinner and I needed to be saved. The Lord Jesus Christ heard my prayer. He forgave my sin and came to live in me. I know He lives in me. I want you to know, He has never failed me. Our God is faithful–trust Him.

WHAT IS THIS THAT GOD HATH DONE UNTO US?

 o you see the Lord in the circumstances of your life? Our God is always at work. It is evident that He allows things to happen in our lives to get our attention. In Genesis chapter forty-two, we find the Lord working in the lives of Joseph's brothers.

The Bible says in Genesis 42:1-28,

> *Now when Jacob saw that there was corn in Egypt, Jacob said unto his sons, Why do ye look one upon another? And he said, Behold, I have heard that there is corn in Egypt: get you down thither, and buy for us from thence; that we may live, and not die. And Joseph's ten brethren went down to buy corn in Egypt. But Benjamin, Joseph's brother, Jacob sent not with his brethren; for he said, Lest peradventure mischief befall him. And the sons of Israel came to buy corn among those that came: for the famine was in the land of*

Canaan. And Joseph was the governor over the land, and he it was that sold to all the people of the land: and Joseph's brethren came, and bowed down themselves before him with their faces to the earth. And Joseph saw his brethren, and he knew them, but made himself strange unto them, and spake roughly unto them; and he said unto them, Whence come ye? And they said, From the land of Canaan to buy food. And Joseph knew his brethren, but they knew not him. And Joseph remembered the dreams which he dreamed of them, and said unto them, Ye are spies; to see the nakedness of the land ye are come. And they said unto him, Nay, my lord, but to buy food are thy servants come. We are all one man's sons; we are true men, thy servants are no spies. And he said unto them, Nay, but to see the nakedness of the land ye are come. And they said, Thy servants are twelve brethren, the sons of one man in the land of Canaan; and, behold, the youngest is this day with our father, and one is not. And Joseph said unto them, That is it that I spake unto you, saying, Ye are spies: hereby ye shall be proved: By the life of Pharaoh ye shall not go forth hence, except your youngest brother come hither. Send one of you, and let him fetch your brother, and ye shall be kept in prison, that your words may be proved, whether there be any truth in you: or else by the life of Pharaoh surely ye are spies. And he put them all together into ward three days. And Joseph said unto them the third day, This do, and live; for I fear God: if ye be true men, let one of your brethren be bound in the house of your prison: go ye, carry corn for the famine of your houses: but bring your youngest brother unto me; so shall your words be verified, and ye shall not die. And they did so. And

they said one to another, We are verily guilty concerning our brother, in that we saw the anguish of his soul, when he besought us, and we would not hear; therefore is this distress come upon us. And Reuben answered them, saying, Spake I not unto you, saying, Do not sin against the child; and ye would not hear? therefore, behold, also his blood is required. And they knew not that Joseph understood them; for he spake unto them by an interpreter. And he turned himself about from them, and wept; and returned to them again, and communed with them, and took from them Simeon, and bound him before their eyes. Then Joseph commanded to fill their sacks with corn, and to restore every man's money into his sack, and to give them provision for the way: and thus did he unto them. And they laded their asses with the corn, and departed thence. And as one of them opened his sack to give his ass provender in the inn, he espied his money; for, behold, it was in his sack's mouth. And he said unto his brethren, My money is restored; and, lo, it is even in my sack: and their heart failed them, and they were afraid, saying one to another, What is this that God hath done unto us?

Note the question in verse twenty-eight, *"What is this that God hath done unto us?"* These fellows said to themselves, "We see God's hand in this. What is He saying to us? What is this work that He is doing? Why is He allowing this to happen to us? We do not understand what is happening, but we know that God is surely in this."

> *God's judgments are acts of love.*

The Lord reminds us again that He deals in the affairs of mankind. I once spoke to a young man who was coming back to God. He told me the story of his life, especially his Christian testimony. He told me how as a teenager he came to know the Lord Jesus as his Savior.

> *The great need in their lives was to be thoroughly right with God, and all these other things were used of God to bring that to pass.*

His parents moved from place to place in this country. He got involved in a church and started serving the Lord. Then something went wrong. He got away from God and away from his family. He joined the Air Force and traveled to England, trying to run from the Lord. When he got to England, he started drinking alcohol and doing other things he should never have done.

He drove by a gas station one day and, of all things, a young lady was working there pumping the gasoline. He started talking to her and after a few days of going by there, he asked her for a date. She said, "I don't go out with fellows who are not Christians." To make a long story short, her father was a Baptist preacher in England, and she was a dedicated Christian. God had taken this young man thousands of miles across the ocean, brought him in an automobile to a gasoline station, and planted a faithful child of God at a gasoline pump to remind him that he needed to turn to the Lord.

He said to me, "It's amazing how God works in the lives of people."

I want to remind you that God is working in the life of every person. You may see Him at work or you may not see Him at work, but God is at work. When Joseph's brothers responded, *"What is this that God hath done unto us?"* they were right on target, because God would soon take these brothers and begin to build the great nation of Israel. They needed to be reminded of the fact that the Lord was at work in their lives.

God Deals With Us in Love

When we think of this question, *"What is this that God hath done unto us?"* let us keep in mind that God always deals with us in love. The Bible says in John 3:16, *"For God so loved the world, that he gave his only begotten Son, that whosoever believeth in him should not perish, but have everlasting life."* We need to establish this one fact very firmly in our thinking, that God deals with us in love. God's judgments are acts of love.

We get the idea at times that God has forsaken us or God is doing something to us that is awful. Some ask, "Lord, why did You allow such a thing to happen to me?" Remember that God is dealing with us in love. Do not allow the Devil to blind you to the goodness of God. The *"goodness of God leadeth thee to repentance"* (Romans 2:4).

God Works to Bring Us to Himself

Something else we must remember is that God's intention is to bring men to Himself. The Bible says in Exodus 19:4, *"Ye have seen what I did unto the Egyptians, and how I bare you on eagles' wings, and brought you unto myself."* As you consider what is going on in your life, in your home, on your job, whatever thoughts are racing through your mind, remember that God is dealing with you in love and His purpose is to bring you to Himself.

God Causes Us to Realize Our Need

Let us look at some very simple things in chapter forty-two of Genesis. First, I want you to see that we must realize our need.

The Bible says in verses one through five,

> *Now when Jacob saw that there was corn in Egypt, Jacob said unto his sons, Why do ye look one upon another? And he said, Behold, I have heard that there is corn in Egypt: get you down thither, and buy for us from thence; that we may live, and not die. And Joseph's ten brethren went down to buy corn in Egypt. But Benjamin, Joseph's brother, Jacob sent not with his brethren; for he said, Lest peradventure mischief befall him. And the sons of Israel came to buy corn among those that came: for the famine was in the land of Canaan.*

There was a famine in the land. There was hunger in the land. A great need had arisen. Jacob, the father of all these men, realized that in order to live they had to eat. Word reached Jacob that there was food down in Egypt. Of all places, Egypt had become the breadbasket for the world during this famine.

Jacob gathered his sons around him and said, "We must do something. There is a great need here and I have heard that there is food down in Egypt. What we must do is send you down to Egypt to get food for us lest we die."

Perhaps at this particular time, they did not see the Lord's hand in the matter, but it was the Lord who had brought about the famine. It was the Lord who allowed Joseph to interpret Pharaoh's dream. It was the Lord who showed Joseph to build granaries in every city and to store the food for the days of famine. The Lord was working in all of this. As the Lord worked, He worked in the life of Jacob and his sons to cause them to realize a real need in their lives. The great need in their lives was to be thoroughly right with God, and all these other things were used of God to bring that to pass.

We are strange creatures–it is only when we realize we have a need that we are moved to action. God works to cause us to realize our need. The Bible says in Psalm 119:67, *"Before I was afflicted I went astray: but now have I kept thy word."* In other words, the psalmist testified that affliction brought him to God. Trouble brought him to the Lord. Problems pointed him to Jesus Christ. Realizing he had a need changed his life. Before he was afflicted, he went astray.

Would it not be wonderful if in all the glory days of our lives, when the sun is shining brightly and everything is going well, we trusted God with all our strength and might and lived for the Lord daily with all the desire possible? But it does not typically happen that way. It is during the days of darkness and the hours of great difficulty, during days of affliction when things go wrong, that we are made to realize we have a need, and we turn our hearts toward the Lord.

Do you realize that we will not grow as Christians; we will not do anything we should do until we realize the great need we have in our lives? Allow God to put His finger on your need. Do you know your need? Christ is all we need!

Allow God to put His finger on your need.

No wonder these brothers said, *"What is this that God hath done unto us?"* The first thing God did was allow a famine and cause them to realize the need. He directed them to Egypt, of all places, because He had a plan for their lives.

GOD REMINDS US OF OUR DEEDS

Try to imagine what was taking place in Egypt. Thousands of people were pouring into Egypt for food. Great hordes of people were going there. Joseph had been appointed by Pharaoh to administrate the dispersing of the food. God had given him wisdom to design a plan. Every city had a place where the people could come to receive the grain that they needed. No doubt there were scores of people filing into Egypt all the time. It was busy, like one of those bazaars we see in certain parts of the world where people are milling about in great masses, trying to purchase goods.

All of this was taking place in the very presence of Joseph, and they thought he could not understand their Hebrew tongue.

Joseph was seated there in the garments of an Egyptian. It had been approximately twenty-five years since he had seen his brethren. There he sat, arrayed like an Egyptian, speaking like an Egyptian, looking like an Egyptian, overseeing all of it, caring for the needs of the people. Suddenly, he lifted his head, and to his amazement, of all people in the world, he saw his brothers coming toward him. What a flood of emotion must have filled his heart and mind! Oh, how he must have felt in that moment to see his brothers after all those years in Egypt.

The Bible says in Genesis 42:6-7, *"And Joseph was the governor over the land, and he it was that sold to all the people of the land: and Joseph's brethren came, and bowed down themselves before him with their faces to the earth. And Joseph saw his brethren, and he knew them,..."*

These three words seem so simple, but think what accompanied this statement, *"...he knew them,..."* Perhaps he thought he would never see them again. He never dreamed that such a moment would come.

The Bible continues, *"...but made himself strange unto them, and spake roughly unto them; and he said unto them, Whence come ye? And they said, From the land of Canaan to buy food."* Remember, Joseph was speaking through an interpreter, but he knew their language. He understood every word they said. His heart was

breaking with every impulse. He was torn apart on the inside. Many emotions were running through his mind. No doubt he thought, "Where's my father? Where is my brother Benjamin?" But he could not burst out with those words. He could not openly let them know who he was, so he spoke roughly to them.

Look closely at what God led Joseph to do. As he spoke to them, the Bible says in verses eight and nine, *"And Joseph knew his brethren, but they knew not him. And Joseph remembered the dreams which he dreamed of them, and said unto them, Ye are spies; to see the nakedness of the land ye are come."*

As you read this chapter, you may wish to mark every time the word *"spies"* occurs. Remember that it was Joseph who approached his brethren as a seventeen-year-old boy in great love, wanting to see them and be with them, bringing them things from their father, checking on them because he loved them. His brethren said falsely to him, "You're just a spy for our father. All you want to do is find out what we are doing and run back and tell our father so he can punish us."

Joseph said, "No, you are mistaken. I love you. That's why I'm here." But again they accused him of being a spy to run and tell on them. Now the table was turned. Their motives were questioned. The very same tactic they used on Joseph, God led Joseph to use on them.

> *After twenty-five years, they could still hear Joseph's voice calling out from that pit!*

The Lord has a special way of reminding us of our deeds. God is a personal God, and He deals with us in a personal way. There are things that trigger my mental processes that do not necessarily trigger yours. Every part of our created makeup is available for God to use. There are even odors I can smell that make me think of incidents in my life as a child.

There are things I can see, words I can hear, and types of people I can witness that make me vividly recall events in my life.

God has a way of reminding every one of us of our deeds. God is reminding you. God is reminding me. God did not start working at this moment in our lives; He has been working for a long time preparing the possibility of our recall.

> *The very same tactic they used on Joseph, God led Joseph to use on them.*

As Joseph spoke roughly to his brethren, he said, "You're spies and you know you are spies." Again they said, "No, no, that's not why we're here. We're here because we are hungry and we need food."

Again Joseph said, "No, you're spies." He drives it home again and again until they are reminded so well of the awful thing they did to their brother.

Is the Lord waking up something in your life? Is God getting your attention again about something you need to remember? Is it painful to think about? Is there something unpleasant you wish you could forget? I will not talk about the forgetting, but rather about the forgiving. God wakes it up so you will bring it to Him and seek His forgiveness.

The Bible continues in verses ten through thirteen, *"And they said unto him, Nay, my lord, but to buy food are thy servants come. We are all one man's sons; we are true men, thy servants are no spies."* Joseph was about to get to something he wanted to hear.

"And he said unto them, Nay, but to see the nakedness of the land ye are come. And they said, Thy servants are twelve brethren,..." That interested Joseph. He was listening very carefully. He wanted to know with all of his heart if his father was still alive and if Benjamin was all right. His heart was beating faster and faster as they spoke.

"...Thy servants are twelve brethren, the sons of one man in the land of Canaan; and, behold, the youngest is this day with our father, and one is not." Think of how Joseph must have felt. His father was still alive and his brother Benjamin was still alive. His heart was leaping with joy. Joseph was reduced in their thinking to, *"...one is not."*

Have you ever gotten news that absolutely thrilled you? The Bible says, *"Behold, the youngest is this day with our father, and one is not."* Little did they know that the one they said *"is not"* was the one with whom they were speaking that day.

Is the Lord waking up something in your life? God wakes it up so you will bring it to Him and seek His forgiveness.

The Bible continues in Genesis 42:14-16,

> *And Joseph said unto them, That is it that I spake unto you, saying, Ye are spies: hereby ye shall be proved: By the life of Pharaoh ye shall not go forth hence, except your youngest brother come hither. Send one of you, and let him fetch your brother, and ye shall be kept in prison, that your words may be proved, whether there be any truth in you: or else by the life of Pharaoh surely ye are spies.*

How many times has God said to you and to me through something He has stirred inside of us, "Here is something you need to care for. Here is something you need to bring to the Lord. Here is something that is wrong and you know it. You need to get it right with God"? How many times has the Lord done that in our lives, and we have done nothing about it?

"What is this that God hath done unto us?" God causes us to realize our need and He reminds us of our deeds. God knows and He causes us to know. We cannot carry these things in our lives that are unforgiven and unconfessed and expect to have God's blessing and God's peace. Therefore He reminds us of our deeds.

GOD WANTS US TO RETURN UNTO HIM

As you search the Scriptures, you will find things in the Word of God that you will not find with only a casual reading. These are very simple things, but they are profound.

> *Do you think you can live long enough to forget your unconfessed sin?*

These men had traveled from the land of Canaan, from the land of God's choosing. Their father was Jacob. Jacob had been told of the promise the true and living God made to Abraham. Abraham had passed it down to Isaac, and Isaac had passed it to Jacob. These sons of Jacob knew about it. They knew there was a God who was real, yet they had traveled to the land of Egypt to a land of many gods and false worshippers. They stood in the court of what they thought was an Egyptian ruler and listened to what he said.

The Bible says that Joseph *"put them all together into ward three days."* He gave them time to think. This is one thing we do not do often. We are in such a rush that it is difficult to give our attention to the Lord. So for three days they were in a prison cell talking to one another. Can you imagine what they talked about? I think I can. In the strangest of circumstances they were considering the only true and living God.

The Bible says in Genesis 42:18, *"And Joseph said unto them the third day, This do, and live;..."* They believed him to be an Egyptian. They thought he was like every other Egyptian. They had been told about the

true and living God, yet Joseph said to them, *"...for I fear God."* When he spoke the name of God, no doubt their hearts were stirred.

They thought they had come to Egypt to talk to an Egyptian. They were the ones who had been taught in the land of Hebron about the true and living God. In light of this, what a startling statement it must have been for this Egyptian ruler to say to them, "I fear your God."

There is no place you can go to get away from God.

What was God doing? The Lord again was driving home to their hearts that they could not escape Him. They could not get away. He is everywhere. This is what the Bible declares.

Psalm 139:1-12 says,

> *O LORD, thou hast searched me, and known me. Thou knowest my downsitting and mine uprising, thou understandest my thought afar off. Thou compassest my path and my lying down, and art acquainted with all my ways. For there is not a word in my tongue, but, lo, O LORD, thou knowest it altogether. Thou hast beset me behind and before, and laid thine hand upon me. Such knowledge is too wonderful for me; it is high, I cannot attain unto it. Whither shall I go from thy spirit? or whither shall I flee from thy presence? If I ascend up into heaven, thou art there: if I make my bed in hell, behold, thou art there. If I take the wings of the morning, and dwell in the uttermost parts of the sea; even there shall thy hand lead me, and thy right hand shall hold me. If I say, Surely the darkness shall cover me; even the night shall be light about me. Yea, the darkness hideth not from thee; but the night shineth as the day: the darkness and the light are both alike to thee.*

There is no place you can go to get away from God. There is no new city to which you can move. There is no new job you can take.

Every part of our created makeup is available for God to use.

There is no new wife you can marry. There is no new place you can go. There is no place to get away from God when God is after you because God wants you to return to Him.

Those men were shaken up. What started out as a trip from home to get some bread to eat had turned into a real ordeal. After twenty-five years, it seemed as if everything they had ever done was running through their minds.

Our story continues. The Bible says in Genesis 42:19-21,

> *If ye be true men, let one of your brethren be bound in the house of your prison: go ye, carry corn for the famine of your houses: but bring your youngest brother unto me; so shall your words be verified, and ye shall not die. And they did so. And they said one to another, We are verily guilty concerning our brother, in that we saw the anguish of his soul, when he besought us, and we would not hear; therefore is this distress come upon us.*

What were they talking about? They were talking about the detailed events of the thing that took place in the life of Joseph more than twenty-five years earlier. They said, "God has never forgotten and God is holding us guilty for what we did to our brother. That's why all of this is happening to us."

How long do you think you can go on? Do you think you can live long enough to forget your unconfessed sin? Where can you go? Where can you hide? There is no escaping God, for He is everywhere.

Consider what Reuben said, *"We are verily guilty concerning our brother, in that we saw the anguish of his soul, when he besought us, and we would not hear; therefore is this distress come upon us."* After twenty-five years, they could still hear Joseph's voice calling out from that pit! Think of that. When God deals with someone, He will let that person know that He is dealing with him.

The Bible says in verse twenty-two, *"And Reuben answered them, saying, Spake I not unto you, saying, Do not sin against the child; and ye would not hear? therefore, behold, also his blood is required."* All of this was taking place in the very presence of Joseph, and they thought he could not understand their Hebrew tongue. God's Word continues in verses twenty-three and twenty-four, *"And they knew not that Joseph understood them; for he spake unto them by an interpreter. And he turned himself about from them, and wept; and returned*

> *The Lord has a special way of reminding us of our needs.*

to them again, and communed with them, and took from them Simeon, and bound him before their eyes." I can hardly read this without weeping.

God was at work. When they got home, they found all their money returned to their sacks. One of them discovered it first. His reply was, "What is this that God hath done unto us?"

The God I know and love and serve is the God who works in the life of every person to bring that person to Himself. *"What is this that God hath done unto us?"* God wants to show us our need, remind us of our deeds, and use those things to bring us to Himself.

Chapter
Seven

HAVE YOU
HAD ENOUGH?

 ittle did Joseph's brothers know when they came to Egypt that the person in charge of everything was their brother Joseph. He had not yet revealed himself to them. But they came to him. When they came, he asked about their father, and he wanted to know if they had any other brothers. They said, "We have a father who is an old man back in the land of Canaan, and we have a brother by the name of Benjamin."

Joseph kept Simeon with him and asked the brothers to go back to the land of Canaan, get their brother Benjamin, and bring him to Egypt. They did not understand his request. They did not know why he asked for such a thing, but they knew they could not come back for food (and they had to have food) unless they brought Benjamin with them.

After much persuasion, they were able to take Benjamin from Jacob and bring him down into Egypt with them and secure the release of Simeon. When chapter forty-three closes in the book of

Genesis, we are at a beautiful banquet in the house of Joseph. Joseph is in one place seated alone. His servants are Egyptians, and they are seated by themselves. And in the same room are the brethren of Joseph, to their amazement, seated in perfect order and feasting in Joseph's house. It would be a wonderful moment right in the midst of that beautiful feast for Joseph to say to his brothers, "I'm Joseph," and tell them the story of how God sent him before them to prepare the way so that they might live. But for a very important reason, Joseph did not take advantage of that opportunity.

As we come to chapter forty-four of the book of Genesis, we wonder why Joseph did not reveal himself to his brethren in chapter forty-three. There was a reason. God was dealing with one of the brothers. God was transforming his life. His name was Judah. Judah was not the oldest. You might think that God would deal with Reuben or with Simeon or with Levi, but God dealt with Judah. God dealt with him in such a way until he finally said, "That's enough! Lord, I surrender."

This is what I want you to see. God does not violate our will, but He does deal with us in such a wonderful fashion in order that we might see His hand in all things and have the opportunity to wave the white flag to Him and say, "Lord, that's enough. I surrender."

Joseph told his brothers that they could go back with plenty. They could go back to their father. He filled their bags, and in filling their bags, he had his steward put his own personal silver cup in Benjamin's bag. Let us take up the story in Genesis 44:1-18,

> *And he commanded the steward of his house, saying, Fill the men's sacks with food, as much as they can carry, and put every man's money in his sack's mouth. And put my cup, the silver cup, in the sack's mouth of the youngest, and his corn money. And he did according to the word that Joseph had spoken. As soon as the morning was light, the men were sent*

away, they and their asses. And when they were gone out of the city, and not yet far off, Joseph said unto his steward, Up, follow after the men; and when thou dost overtake them, say unto them, Wherefore have ye rewarded evil for good? Is not this it in which my lord drinketh, and whereby indeed he divineth? ye have done evil in so doing. And he overtook them, and he spake unto them these same words. And they said unto him, Wherefore saith my lord these words? God forbid that thy servants should do according to this thing: Behold, the money, which we found in our sacks' mouths, we brought again unto thee out of the land of Canaan: how then should we steal out of thy lord's house silver or gold? With whomsoever of thy servants it be found, both let him die, and we also will be my lord's bondmen. And he said, Now also let it be according unto your words: he with whom it is found shall be my servant; and ye shall be blameless. Then they speedily took down every man his sack to the ground, and opened every man his sack. And he searched, and began at the eldest, and left at the youngest: and the cup was found in Benjamin's sack. Then they rent their clothes, and laded every man his ass, and returned to the city. And Judah and his brethren came to Joseph's house; for he was yet there: and they fell before him on the ground. And Joseph said unto them, What deed is this that ye have done? wot ye not that such a man as I can certainly divine? And Judah said, What shall we say unto my lord? what shall we speak? or how shall we clear ourselves? God hath found out the iniquity of thy servants: behold, we are my lord's servants, both we, and he also with whom the cup is found. And he said, God forbid that I should do so: but the man in whose

hand the cup is found, he shall be my servant; and as for you, get you up in peace unto your father. Then Judah came near unto him, and said, Oh my lord, let thy servant, I pray thee, speak a word in my lord's ears, and let not thine anger burn against thy servant: for thou art even as Pharaoh.

Notice what Judah said to Joseph. The Word of God records his statement in verse sixteen. Judah was at his wit's end. He did not understand everything that had happened. He had no way to explain

> God wants to bring us to the place where we are willing to do whatever He desires.

how the cup got into Benjamin's sack. He did not know all the details. He could have thrown up his hands and said, "Why is all this going on?" But he realized God was in it and he said, *"What shall we say unto my lord? what shall we speak? or how shall we clear ourselves? God hath found out the iniquity of thy servants."*

Judah declared, "In all of this, I can see that God has dealt with me, and I am willing to surrender to the Lord. That is enough. I surrender."

Remember that back in Ur of the Chaldees, God found a man by the name of Abraham. He promised Abraham a seed and a land. God made a covenant with Abraham that He would make of him a great nation.

How could God promise such a thing without a son? When Abraham was a hundred years old, God gave him a son, Isaac. Isaac had sons, Jacob and Esau. Of those two sons, God chose the son Jacob. Jacob had twelve sons. One of those sons was to form the tribe from which the Lord Jesus Christ would eventually come. That tribe was the tribe of Judah. Our Lord is referred to as *"the Lion of the tribe of Juda"* (Revelation 5:5).

God had something for all those men. God had something He was going to do with each of their lives. But the Lord had something unusual for the tribe of Judah. God singled out Judah. God separated Judah from his brethren. God was going to do something above the ordinary with Judah.

In Genesis 49:8, as Jacob was dying and blessing his sons, the Bible says, *"Judah, thou art he whom thy brethren shall praise: thy hand shall be in the neck of thine enemies; thy father's children shall bow down before thee."* He was not the oldest. The order of the sons of Jacob was Reuben, followed by Simeon, Levi, then Judah. Jacob continues in verses nine and ten,

> *Judah is a lion's whelp: from the prey, my son, thou art gone up: he stooped down, he couched as a lion, and as an old lion; who shall rouse him up? The sceptre shall not depart from Judah, nor a lawgiver from between his feet, until Shiloh come; and unto him shall the gathering of the people be.*

"Shiloh" means "rest." This is one of the names used for our Lord Jesus. He is our rest. God revealed to Jacob that Judah was the son who would form the tribe from which the Lord Jesus Christ, the promised Savior, would come.

God does not reveal things to us until we are ready to receive them.

Let us understand why God put chapter forty-four in the book of Genesis. It would have been just as easy for Joseph to reveal himself to his brethren in the closing part of chapter forty-three while in the banquet hall of his own house. But God does not reveal things to us until we are ready to receive them.

God is not going to do the things in our lives that He desires to do until we are ready to receive them. Our Lord has such wonderful

things for us. However, He cannot bless us with those things until He makes us ready to receive them. God worked in the life of Judah so that he was ready to receive God's blessings.

GOD DEALS WITH INDIVIDUALS

Here was a family of twelve boys, and God was dealing with all of them. But in a special way, He dealt with one of them. God deals with individuals.

We may speak collectively of a church, and we may talk about God working in that church. But we must remember that when God works in a church, He works in the lives of individuals in that church. When God is going to do a work, He begins that work by working in the heart of one human being. God works in the lives of individuals.

I have a family. I love my family collectively as a unit, but I also love them individually. God deals with families. But when God works in the family, He works through the heart of an individual.

You may work on a job, and perhaps there are many people at that work place. God wants to be glorified on your job. But how does God get glory on that job? He gets glory through working in the lives of individual employees on that job. God works in the hearts of individuals.

I could tell you so many stories to illustrate this, but I am thinking of one in particular. I was standing one day talking to a lady at her door about knowing Christ as her Savior. I knew there were other people in the home, and it would have been altogether proper for me to go inside because she was not alone, but she preferred that I speak to her about the Savior at her door.

As I talked to her and explained to her the way of salvation, we came to the point of praying to receive Christ as Savior. I asked her if she would trust the Lord Jesus as her personal Savior. She bowed her head, asked God to forgive her sin, and by faith received Christ as Savior.

When I finished talking, suddenly a young teenage girl stepped from behind the door. I had no way of knowing she had been standing there. She had heard every word I had spoken and said, "Would it be all right if I trusted the Lord Jesus as my Savior too?" I am saying that God has a way of working in the heart and life of each individual.

GOD'S WAYS ARE NOT OUR WAYS

We also see in this story that God's ways are not our ways. In Isaiah 55:8-9 the Word of God says, *"For my thoughts are not your thoughts, neither are your ways my ways, saith the LORD. For as the heavens are higher than the earth, so are my ways higher than your ways, and my thoughts than your thoughts."*

I can testify to this fact; I know this to be true. There are many times I know what God is going to do, but I marvel to see how He gets it done.

> *God worked to make a self-willed, stubborn man who looked out only for himself and his own, into the kind of man that said, "I would rather live the rest of my life in bondage than to see my father's heart broken and my brother living in slavery."*

The Lord took one of Jacob's sons, Judah, and made him a prince. From his loins he formed a tribe, and from that tribe, the Lord Jesus Christ came into this world. However, we are surprised to see the one He uses.

In Genesis chapter thirty-seven, Joseph had been thrown into the pit. Reuben wanted to spare his life. I think Reuben had in the back of his mind that he wanted to scare the boy and get him back to his father. But suddenly, in Genesis 37:26-27 the Bible says, *"And Judah said unto his brethren, What profit is it if we slay our brother, and conceal his blood? Come, and let us sell him to the Ishmeelites, and let not our hand be upon him; for he is our brother and our flesh. And his brethren were content."*

Judah said, "He's our brother; he's our flesh. We don't want to hurt him but let's sell him and get rid of him." These are such contradictory statements. Judah said, "He's our brother, but let's sell him. We don't want to hurt him, but let's get rid of him. He's our flesh, but let's make a slave out of him." Judah said those things.

Let us consider a chapter in the Bible that we often skip because it contains such a bad story. In chapter thirty-eight of Genesis, Judah had a child by his own daughter-in-law. He mistook her for a harlot. I am trying to tell you that God's ways are not our ways. I am not saying that God was in favor of Judah and his daughter-in-law in their awful act, but I am saying that in spite of everything we think, God is able to work.

There are people who think, "With what I've done, the mistakes I've made, how can God ever do anything with my life?" God is able.

GOD DESIRES TO BRING US
TO THE PLACE OF SURRENDER

As we read chapter forty-four of Genesis, we find a different man than the Judah we found in chapter thirty-eight. He is now a broken man. He is a man who has come to the place in his life where he is surrendered. Why does God allow this one last event to take place?

Why did Joseph not reveal himself in chapter forty-three? Because God is doing one last thing in the life of Judah so he will yield to the Lord.

Remember in chapter forty-two when Judah went back to his father Jacob and said, *"The man, who is the lord of the land,…said unto us,…bring your youngest brother unto me: then shall I know that ye are no spies."* And Jacob said, *"My son shall not go down with you; for his brother is dead, and he is left alone: if mischief befall him by the way in the which ye go, then shall ye bring down my gray hairs with sorrow to the grave."*

Judah said, *"I will be surety for him; of my hand shalt thou require him: if I bring him not unto thee, and set him before thee, then let me bear the blame for ever."*

The Word of God says that when Judah came back he was at the place of surrender. Notice the language of the Bible. The Word of God says in Genesis 44:14, *"And Judah and his brethren came to Joseph's house; for he was yet there: and they fell before him on the ground."*

They were so sure that no one had done anything wrong, they were so sure that the cup was not in anyone's bag, that they speedily emptied all their bags. But they found that something was wrong. They rushed back to Joseph's house, and they fell on the floor before Joseph. The Bible continues in verses fifteen and sixteen,

> *And Joseph said unto them, What deed is this that ye have done? wot ye not that such a man as I can certainly divine? And Judah said, What shall we say unto my lord? what shall we speak? or how shall we clear ourselves? God hath found out the iniquity of thy servants: behold, we are my lord's servants, both we, and he also with whom the cup is found.*

Judah was a broken man. Do you know where God wants to bring you and me? God wants to bring us to the place where we are willing to do whatever He desires. He is not going to force us, but God wants us to be willing to yield to Him. Have you trusted Him as your Savior? Do you know that you have given Christ your heart and life? Have you yielded to Him? Have you asked God to forgive your sin? By faith have you received Him as your Savior? If not, you can trust Him now.

As a Christian, do you realize that God is dealing with you in one way after another? You may say, "God is dealing with Joseph." Right, but God dealt with Judah by dealing with Joseph. It is not always something that happens to you. It could be happening around you, to someone you know and love, but God is still speaking to you. He is speaking to that person also, but God is speaking to you. He wants to bring us to the place where we say, "That's enough, Lord. You don't need to do anymore. I surrender."

OUR LIVES AFFECT OTHERS

I want you to understand that our lives affect others. One of the most passionate things you will ever read anywhere is the speech Judah made to Joseph as he pleaded to Joseph on behalf of his brother Benjamin. Judah said in Genesis 44:31-33,

> It shall come to pass, when he seeth that the lad is not with us, that he will die: and thy servants shall bring down the gray hairs of thy servant our father with sorrow to the grave. For thy servant became surety for the lad unto my father, saying, If I bring him not unto thee, then I shall bear the blame to my father for ever. Now therefore, I pray thee, let thy servant abide instead of the lad a bondman to my lord; and let the lad go up with his brethren.

This is not the same man who went back and lied to his father about Joseph. He is not the same man who told Jacob that Joseph had been ripped apart by a wild beast. This is not the same man who broke his father's heart. This is not the same man who with his own hands separated Joseph from the rest of his brethren and sent him into slavery. He had the same name and he looked the same, but God had changed his heart. He said, "I cannot bear to think that my father will have a broken heart and my brother Benjamin will be separated from our family."

Judah had been a selfish, self-willed man. If we look closely, we will see that many of us are the same way. Like Judah, we need to come to the place where we realize that the actions of our lives affect others. Others are hurt by our stubbornness and selfishness. What a tragedy!

It is wonderful to know that God can make a life over again. God can change people. God worked to make a self-willed, stubborn man who looked out only for himself and his own, into the kind of man that said, "I would rather live the rest of my life in bondage than to see my father's heart broken and my brother living in slavery." God is able to change people's lives. God changed Judah, and He is able to bring us to the place where we say, "Lord, I've had enough. I surrender all to Thee."

Chapter Eight

YOU SOLD ME, BUT GOD SENT ME

 n spite of all that Joseph had been through, he realized that God was working in his life. "Y*e sold me*" but *"God did send me."* God wants to bring every one of us to the place where we remove all secondary causes and see Him at work in our lives.

The Bible says in Genesis 45:1-5,

> *Then Joseph could not refrain himself before all them that stood by him; and he cried, Cause every man to go out from me. And there stood no man with him, while Joseph made himself known unto his brethren. And he wept aloud: and the Egyptians and the house of Pharaoh heard. And Joseph said unto his brethren, I am Joseph; doth my father yet live? And his brethren could not answer him; for they were troubled at his presence. And Joseph said unto his brethren, Come near to me, I pray you. And they came near.*

And he said, I am Joseph your brother, whom ye sold into Egypt. Now therefore be not grieved, nor angry with yourselves, that ye sold me hither: for God did send me before you to preserve life.

When Joseph saw that Judah was a broken man, he could not refrain himself. He caused all others to go out and he made himself known to his brothers. Joseph explained to them, "Do not be troubled because you sold me into Egypt. God was working during that terrible time. You sold me, but God sent me."

God wants to bring every one of us to the place where we remove all secondary causes and see Him at work in our lives.

Joseph wanted his brothers to know, "When you handed me over to those merchantmen, those were really God's hands that gave me to those merchantmen. When that woman came after me, and I ran and left my coat, it was God who allowed me to go to prison. And when I went to prison and met the butler and the baker, it was God who put me there and gave me favor with the jailor. When I was forgotten for two years, it was God who caused me not to be remembered, because in the moment that I needed to be remembered, when Pharaoh had a dream, then I was called to interpret the dream. I see through eyes of faith that God's hand was in it all, and I realize that you sold me, but it was God who sent me. All secondary causes are removed and I see God in it all."

The prophet Jonah came to the same place of faith in God. He told the sailors that he was the problem, and they threw him overboard. With their own hands, they threw him overboard. However, in the second chapter of Jonah, verse three, he told the Lord in his prayer, *"For thou hadst cast me into the deep, in the midst of the seas."* He was saying, "Lord, You threw me overboard, not the sailors."

It was the sailors who took hold of him, lifted him up, and threw him into the sea, but he said, "Really, it was God who did it."

We must come to the place by faith where we remove all secondary causes and understand how God has been in the twists and turns of our lives. With just one different little twist or turn, we could be a thousand miles from where we are today.

By the time I was in the third grade, I had lived in nineteen different places. My father and mother's marriage finally ended in divorce. I look back across my life, and the only way I can explain it is, God was with me.

All secondary causes are removed, and I see God in it all. You can deal with your life when you come to that. You can forgive people when you come to that place by faith.

Joseph truly forgave his brothers for the sin they had committed against him. He did not live his life with bitterness in

The principle of forgiveness put to practice means that you never come to the place where you are unwilling to forgive others.

his heart. You may ask, "How was he able to forgive?" The Lord enabled him to forgive because he saw by faith that God was in every circumstance. He said, "You sold me, but God sent me."

THE PRINCIPLE OF FORGIVENESS

Joseph knew what it meant to forgive, do you? The Bible says in Ephesians 4:32, *"And be ye kind one to another, tenderhearted, forgiving one another, even as God for Christ's sake hath forgiven you."* The great principle of forgiveness is, *"Even as God for Christ's sake hath forgiven you."*

You may not think that someone deserves to be forgiven, but that is not the point. Why do you think God has forgiven you? He did not forgive you because you deserved forgiveness. The Bible says, *"Even as God for Christ's sake hath forgiven you."* We did not earn our forgiveness. We did not merit our forgiveness. Jesus Christ purchased all of that on the cross.

> *Joseph wanted his brothers to know, "When you handed me over to those merchantmen, those were really God's hands that gave me to those merchantmen."*

When we come to the Lord and ask God to forgive our sin and by faith trust Christ as Savior, God can forgive us because Christ has paid our sin debt. There is a principle here that God forgives us, and we are to forgive others *"even as God for Christ's sake hath forgiven"* us. The principle is that I am to forgive others because I have been forgiven.

What does it mean to forgive? To forgive meant that Joseph was willing to treat his brothers as if they had never done anything wrong to him. Joseph was willing to treat his brothers as if they had never planned and schemed to throw him into the pit, had never threatened to kill him, and had never sold him to the merchantmen who carried him as a slave down to Egypt. It meant that he was willing to live before them and with them as if they had never committed one sinful act against him. It meant that all the rough, ugly things that could have stood between Joseph and his brethren were forgiven. He was willing to say, "Those things, as far as I am concerned, don't exist. You don't ever need to mention them again." He was willing to live his life as if those brothers had never done one thing to harm him. This is what it means to forgive someone.

THE PRINCIPLE PUT TO PRACTICE

In Matthew chapter eighteen, the Lord talks about forgiveness. Over and over He mentions faults and forgiveness, and His disciples are listening. The Bible says in Matthew 18:21, *"Then came Peter to him, and said, Lord, how oft shall my brother sin against me, and I forgive him?"* Then he answers his own question. He must have thought, "Lord, I already know the answer, so I'm going to ask the question and then give You the answer." But he did not really know the answer. He asked, *"Till seven times?"* I am sure Peter thought that sounded good. Verse twenty-two continues, *"Jesus saith unto him, I say not unto thee, Until seven times: but, Until seventy times seven."* If you are trying to do the math, your answer is 490. Then if after the 490th time, you do not forgive, that is not what Christ is talking about. The principle of forgiveness put to practice means that you never come to the place where you are unwilling to forgive others. You always forgive.

If there is someone in your life you have not forgiven, you are stopping the blessing of God. Joseph could have had all these things happen to him and hated every day of his life. But when you can see the Lord in things and look to Him, you can put this principle into practice.

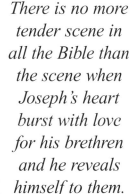

There is no more tender scene in all the Bible than the scene when Joseph's heart burst with love for his brethren and he reveals himself to them.

THE POWER TO FORGIVE

Where does the power to forgive come from? It is not your power. Can the Lord Jesus forgive? Yes. Then where do you think we get the power to forgive? We find this power in the Lord Jesus Christ.

The Bible says in John 15:1-5,

> *I am the true vine, and my Father is the husbandman. Every branch in me that beareth not fruit he taketh away: and every branch that beareth fruit, he purgeth it, that it may bring forth more fruit. Now ye are clean through the word which I have spoken unto you. Abide in me, and I in you. As the branch cannot bear fruit of itself, except it abide in the vine; no more can ye, except ye abide in me. I am the vine, ye are the branches: He that abideth in me, and I in him, the same bringeth forth much fruit: for without me ye can do nothing.*

If you are a Christian and you say you cannot forgive, there is only one reason. The reason you cannot forgive is that you are not abiding in Christ, giving Him the place in your life He richly deserves. This is how Joseph was able to forgive his brethren and live with them as if they had never sinned against him.

The branch only brings forth what the vine produces. We try to live and forgive and get along as branches without the vine. The branch can only bring forth what the vine produces. The Lord Jesus says in verse seven, *"If ye abide in me, and my words abide in you, ye shall ask what ye will, and it shall be done unto you."*

> *To forgive meant that Joseph was willing to treat his brothers as if they had never done anything wrong to him.*

God's Word says in John 15:8-10, *"Herein is my Father glorified, that ye bear much fruit; so shall ye be my disciples. As the Father hath loved me, so have I loved you: continue ye in my love. If ye keep my commandments, ye shall abide in my love;..."* How can I do this? How can I treat people as the Lord Jesus would treat them? The only way I can do this is to be so full of Christ that He loves them through me.

Verses ten through twelve say,

> *If ye keep my commandments, ye shall abide in my love; even as I have kept my Father's commandments, and abide in his love. These things have I spoken unto you, that my joy might remain in you, and that your joy might be full. This is my commandment, That ye love one another, as I have loved you.*

The Lord Jesus said, *"This is my commandment, That ye love one another."* How do we love the unlovely? The power to do this comes only from the Lord Jesus. He is our source. He is our enabler. He is the Vine; we are the branches. As Christians, we have a spiritual relationship with God that enables us to deal with people in a Christlike way.

The principle is that I am to forgive others because I have been forgiven.

Our Lord says in verses sixteen and seventeen,

> *Ye have not chosen me, but I have chosen you, and ordained you, that ye should go and bring forth fruit, and that your fruit should remain: that whatsoever ye shall ask of the Father in my name, he may give it you. These things I command you, that ye love one another.*

May we all seek to have the relationship with Jesus Christ that we so desperately need, for it is only through Him that we have the power to forgive others and to love the unlovely in this world. He has demonstrated to us what it truly means to be forgiven, and it is only in Him that we find the strength to forgive. Joseph found

strength in the Lord to forgive and in faith to say, "You sold me, but God sent me." There is no more tender scene in all the Bible than the scene when Joseph's heart burst with love for his brethren and he revealed himself to them. Oh, how God was glorified in Joseph's action! His desire for them to know him could only be satisfied when they were prepared to receive him.

Chapter Nine

STOP AND THANK THE LORD

s we reach chapter forty-six of the book of Genesis, we see that it had been a long, hard road for Jacob. The heartache that he had known had been severe. He had lived with the awful thought that his precious son Joseph had been torn apart by wild beasts. Recently, he had been separated from his son Simeon and also from Benjamin. His heart was very heavy.

Like any father, when his sons were gone, he was looking every day for their return, waiting for them to come home. They had told him that the only way they could go back to Egypt to get any food was for everyone to go back. He had no idea what was going on; he could only imagine. He was looking for their return. One day he saw them coming. They were not simply coming home; they were coming to get him and take him with them back to Egypt.

Years before, as a seventeen-year-old boy, Joseph was sold by his brothers as a slave to merchantmen traveling to Egypt.

In the providence of God, Joseph found himself in the house of Potiphar, one of Pharaoh's powerful captains.

When Jacob got to Beersheba, he got out of those fancy wagons and got on his face in the dirt and said, "Before I go any farther, before I leave this land, as eager as I am to see my son Joseph, as rapid as my heart beats with the joyful thought of seeing his face, I am going to thank the Lord for making this possible."

In Potiphar's house, Joseph ran into some difficulty. Potiphar's wife lied about him. Potiphar, angry because of his wife's lies, had Joseph thrown into prison. There Joseph waited for God to move and work in his life.

Just at the right time, Pharaoh had a dream, and he was told by one of his servants of an acquaintance he had while in prison. His name was Joseph, and he could interpret dreams.

Joseph was brought from prison to stand before the Pharaoh to interpret his dream. God gave Joseph an opportunity to save the entire land of Egypt and actually to become a type of savior for the world because of the far-reaching famine. Egypt became a breadbasket for the world because of the plan that God gave Joseph. God revealed to Joseph that there would be seven years of plenty and then seven years of famine.

During the years of plenty, Joseph had storehouses prepared in every city in Egypt so that the people could come to those places to get food. After the people exhausted their money, their lands were taken and then they gave themselves as servants to Pharaoh.

In the meantime, the famine touched the land of Canaan where Joseph's brothers and father were living. They heard there was bread in Egypt. They made the trip to Egypt. Eventually Joseph revealed himself to his brethren. We read in Genesis 45:4-5,

> *And Joseph said unto his brethren, Come near to me, I pray you. And they came near. And he said, I am Joseph your brother, whom ye sold into Egypt. Now therefore be not grieved, nor angry with yourselves, that ye sold me hither: for God did send me before you to preserve life.*

As he revealed himself to his brethren, they rejoiced together, but Joseph longed to see his father.

Pharaoh heard that Joseph's brethren had come. When the news reached Pharaoh, he said to Joseph, "I want you to prepare wagons in a kingly fashion and send them back to Canaan to fetch your father and bring him down here with us. We are going to give you the best of the land of Egypt. We are going to reward you for what you have done."

The Word of God says in Genesis 45:27-46:7,

> *And they told him all the words of Joseph, which he had said unto them: and when he saw the wagons which Joseph had sent to carry him, the spirit of Jacob their father revived: and Israel said, It is enough; Joseph my son is yet alive: I will go and see him before I die. And Israel took his journey with all that he had, and came to Beer-sheba, and offered sacrifices unto the God of his father Isaac. And God spake unto Israel in the visions of the night, and said, Jacob, Jacob. And he said, Here am I. And he said, I am God, the God of thy father: fear not to go down into Egypt; for I will there make of thee a great nation: I will go down with*

*thee into Egypt; and I will also surely bring thee up
again: and Joseph shall put his hand upon thine eyes.
And Jacob rose up from Beer-sheba: and the sons of
Israel carried Jacob their father, and their little ones,
and their wives, in the wagons which Pharaoh had sent
to carry him. And they took their cattle, and their
goods, which they had gotten in the land of Canaan,
and came into Egypt, Jacob, and all his seed with him:
his sons, and his sons' sons with him, his daughters,
and his sons' daughters, and all his seed brought he
with him into Egypt.*

Notice carefully what happened in verse one of chapter forty-six.
On Jacob's way to Egypt, he stopped at Beersheba and offered
sacrifices to God. I am certain Jacob was very eager to see Joseph,
but he took the time to stop and properly thank the Lord. Let us not
forget to thank the Lord. Our gratitude to God or lack of it reveals
the place our Lord holds in our lives.

WE SHOULD SEE THE BLESSINGS

Imagine the anguish Jacob was under when his sons were all
gone. He was left in Hebron alone. Joseph had been taken from him
years before. One of his older sons, Simeon, had been taken from
him because this man in Egypt had insisted that he stay until
Benjamin was brought to Egypt.

After much persuading, especially by Judah, Jacob allowed
Benjamin to go down into Egypt. He did not want to lose any more
of his sons, but he especially did not want anything to happen to
Benjamin. Jacob must have been going through much anguish as he
thought about his boys and wondered where they were, what they
were doing, and when they would be home.

Suddenly, he saw them coming. They told him that Joseph was alive, but he had trouble believing it. Let us continue the story in Genesis 45:17-27,

> *And Pharaoh said unto Joseph, Say unto thy brethren, This do ye; lade your beasts, and go, get you unto the land of Canaan; and take your father and your households, and come unto me: and I will give you the good of the land of Egypt, and ye shall eat the fat of the land. Now thou art commanded, this do ye; take you wagons out of the land of Egypt for your little ones, and for your wives, and bring your father, and come. Also regard not your stuff; for the good of all the land of Egypt is yours. And the children of Israel did so: and Joseph gave them wagons, according to the commandment of Pharaoh, and gave them provision for the way. To all of them he gave each man changes of raiment; but to Benjamin he gave three hundred pieces of silver, and five changes of raiment. And to his father he sent after this manner; ten asses laden with the good things of Egypt, and ten she asses laden with corn and bread and meat for his father by the way. So he sent his brethren away, and they departed: and he said unto them, See that ye fall not out by the way. And they went up out of Egypt, and came into the land of Canaan unto Jacob their father, and told him, saying, Joseph is yet alive, and he is governor over all the land of Egypt. And Jacob's heart fainted, for he believed them not. And they told him all the words of Joseph, which he had said unto them: and when he saw the wagons which Joseph had sent to carry him, the spirit of Jacob their father revived.*

When Jacob saw the wagons, he saw the blessings. He recognized what had been done for him, and this did something wonderful for his heart.

Our gratitude to God should bring about obedience to God. Obedience to God is not simply doing His will; it is delighting in doing His will.

The Devil works hard to blind us to the goodness of God. He tries to blind us to what God has done for us. He wants us to see only the burdens and never the blessings, to see all the trouble and none of the victories. The Devil has a way of trying to blind us to anything that is good, especially in the midst of our problems.

When Jacob saw those wagons, as they came in such a kingly fashion, they confirmed that the story he had been told was true. When he saw the wagons, the Bible says his spirit was revived. He recognized the hand of God.

As we see the blessings, God does a work in our hearts. He refreshes us by His Spirit, and He speaks to us. We need to stop and see the blessings. We see God's blessings as we look to the Lord Jesus.

WE SHOULD THANK OUR GOD

Jacob thanked the Lord. Notice what the Bible says in verse one of chapter forty-six, *"And Israel took his journey with all that he had, and came to Beer-sheba, and offered sacrifices unto the God of his father Isaac."* He thanked God.

As we think of the land of Canaan, we understand that Beersheba is at the southern tip of the land. From Hebron to Beersheeba is about twenty-five or thirty miles. I do not know how long it would have taken them to travel that distance in their wagons.

But when they reached the southern tip of the land, before they ever went out of the Promised Land, before they left Canaan, Jacob said, "Stop the wagons. I know we are in a hurry to get to Egypt. I know we are excited about seeing Joseph, but there is something more important than seeing Joseph. We must thank the Lord!"

What could have been more important than seeing Joseph? The thing that was more important was thanking the God who made it possible to see Joseph. So they put a halt to everything. The old man got out of the wagon, got on his face before God, and thanked the Lord. Before he started into the desert on the way to Egypt at the southern tip of the border of his land, the Bible says he offered sacrifices to the God of his father Isaac.

There is a world of difference between thinking about the Lord and actually thanking the Lord. Thanking God is not simply thinking, "Well, this came from the Lord. Isn't God good?" We must take the time from everything else to thank the Lord, to call out to God and say, "Lord, we know this came from You and we want to thank You for it."

When Jacob got to Beersheba, he got out of those fancy wagons and got on his face in the dirt and said, "Before I go any farther, before I leave this land, as eager as I am to see my son Joseph, as rapid as my heart beats with the joyful thought of seeing his face, I am going to thank the Lord for making this possible."

> *Jacob said, "Stop the wagons. I know we are in a hurry to get to Egypt. I know we are excited about seeing Joseph, but there is something more important that seeing Joseph. We must thank the Lord!"*

All of us who have children recall the days of trying to teach our children to say "thank you." Over and over again we would teach them, "When someone gives you something, does something kind for you, or complements you, we want you to say 'thank you.'"

To forgive meant that Joseph was willing to treat his brothers as if they had never done anything wrong to him.

We would stand and watch as they were presented gum, candy, or a gift. If they did not say "thank you," we would rush quickly to them and ask, "What are you supposed to say?" Then they would say after a little coaxing, "Thank you." And we would say, "That's right." We hoped the day would come when they would be given things and would not have to be coaxed to say thank you.

I wonder how many times God has hovered near us when we have been absolutely showered with His blessings and we have not said, "Thank You, Lord, for all You have done." We must not forget to thank the Lord for His goodness in our lives.

WE SHOULD OBEY THE LORD

The Bible says in Genesis 46:2-4,

And God spake unto Israel in the visions of the night, and said, Jacob, Jacob. And he said, Here am I. And he said, I am God, the God of thy father: fear not to go down into Egypt; for I will there make of thee a great nation: I will go down with thee into Egypt; and I will also surely bring thee up again: and Joseph shall put his hand upon thine eyes.

COURAGE

Do you see what God did for Jacob? God gave him courage. Notice what He said in verse three, *"I am God, the God of thy father: fear not to go down into Egypt;..."* He gave him courage. Courage comes from our faith in God. God said to Jacob, *"Fear not to go down into Egypt."*

ASSURANCE

Notice what else God did. The Word of God says He gave Jacob assurance. He said, *"...for I will there make of thee a great nation:..."* He said, "I am going to be with you. You don't have to go alone. I am going to help you. I am going to stand with you. I will be with you."

Some of us are afraid of more things than we would like to admit. God said to Jacob, "I want you to know that you do not have to be afraid. I am going to give you courage. I want you to know that you do not have to go alone. I am going with you."

We must claim this promise in our own lives. God promises us that He will be with us. We do not have to live the Christian life alone. He promises to walk with us.

DIRECTION

Notice something else the Word of God says. The Lord gives direction. Verse four says, *"I will go down with thee into Egypt; and I will also surely bring thee up again: and Joseph shall put his hand upon thine eyes."* Jacob was told for sure that he would see Joseph and that Joseph's hand would reach out to touch his eyes.

Some of us say, "I see God working in my life. I see the blessings." If we know that God is blessing our lives, we should obey Him. You may say, "I have thanked the Lord for my salvation and for His goodness in my life." That is good, but what about following through and obeying the Lord by doing what He wants you to do? If we are truly thankful for what God is doing in our lives, it will make a difference in how we live. Our gratitude to God should bring about obedience to God. Obedience to God is not simply doing His will; it is delighting in doing His will. Are you delighting in doing His will?

The Devil works hard to blind us to the goodness of God.

There is no doubt that God wants us to see the evidence of His blessings in our lives. He desires for us to see His blessings so that we might have a grateful heart for what He has done. He wants us to thank Him and obey Him.

THE PRECIOUS MOMENTS IN LIFE

 s we look at the life of Joseph, we come to the moment in time when Joseph and his father Jacob were reunited. This stands out as one of the precious moments in the life of Joseph and one of the most tender moments recorded in the Bible.

In Genesis chapter forty-six we find the record of Jacob and his family entering into Egypt. Consider the names of the sons of Jacob. The Bible says in verse eight, *"And these are the names of the children of Israel, which came into Egypt, Jacob and his sons: Reuben, Jacob's firstborn."* Remember the names of these sons of Jacob:

Verse nine says, *"And the sons of Reuben;..."*

Verse ten says, *"And the sons of Simeon;..."*

Verse eleven says, *"And the sons of Levi;..."*

Verse twelve says, *"And the sons of Judah;..."*

Verse thirteen says, *"And the sons of Issachar;..."*

Verse fourteen says, *"And the sons of Zebulun;..."*

Verse sixteen says, *"And the sons of Gad;..."*

Verse seventeen says, *"And the sons of Asher;..."*

Verse twenty says, *"And unto Joseph in the land of Egypt were born Manasseh and Ephraim,..."*

Verse twenty-one says, *"And the sons of Benjamin..."*

Verse twenty-three says, *"And the sons of Dan;..."*

Verse twenty-four says, *"And the sons of Naphtali;..."*

Here we see the sons of Jacob coming into the land of Egypt with their families. The Bible says in verses twenty-six and twenty-seven,

> *All the souls that came with Jacob into Egypt, which came out of his loins, besides Jacob's sons' wives, all the souls were threescore and six; and the sons of Joseph, which were born him in Egypt, were two souls: all the souls of the house of Jacob, which came into Egypt, were threescore and ten.*

God gives us this account because these seventy souls and their descendants would form the nation of Israel, the nation through which God would bless the entire world.

The Word of God continues in Genesis 46:28-34,

> *And he sent Judah before him unto Joseph, to direct his face unto Goshen; and they came into the land of Goshen. And Joseph made ready his chariot, and went up to meet Israel his father, to Goshen, and presented himself unto him; and he fell on his neck, and wept on his neck a good while. And Israel said*

unto Joseph, Now let me die, since I have seen thy face, because thou art yet alive. And Joseph said unto his brethren, and unto his father's house, I will go up, and shew Pharaoh, and say unto him, My brethren, and my father's house, which were in the land of Canaan, are come unto me; and the men are shepherds, for their trade hath been to feed cattle; and they have brought their flocks, and their herds, and all that they have. And it shall come to pass, when Pharaoh shall call you, and shall say, What is your occupation? That ye shall say, Thy servants' trade hath been about cattle from our youth even until now, both we, and also our fathers: that ye may dwell in the land of Goshen; for every shepherd is an abomination unto the Egyptians.

Take special note of an expression in verse twenty-nine of Genesis chapter forty-six. The Bible says, *"And Joseph made ready his chariot, and went up to meet Israel his father, to Goshen, and presented himself unto him; and he fell on his neck, and wept on his neck a good while."* Prayerfully meditate upon these last three words of the verse, *"a good while."*

Live your life in such a way that you leave no room for doubt concerning your faith in God.

I do not know how long *"a good while"* is, but I know it is *"a good while."* I like the language God has chosen to use here. What a precious moment! Joseph was reunited with his father and wept on his neck *"a good while."*

When I was just a boy, my father died. That was an extremely sad day in my life. He died on Easter Sunday. My mother announced to me that we were going to take my father's body from Tennessee where we were living to bury him in Alabama, the place of his birth.

We drove to Selma, Alabama, to the New Live Oak Cemetery to have a graveside service for my father. I was in my early teens. Meeting us at the graveside was my father's only living brother. His name was Clarence Sexton. I was named after my Uncle Clarence.

> *If you marry someone who has never learned to honor his parents, that person will not show the respect that he has the God-given responsibility of showing to you.*

When the graveside service was concluded, the family left and my uncle returned to his home in Tuscaloosa, Alabama. That was the last time I saw him until I became a man.

After I was married, my wife and I decided that we were going to go to Alabama to find my uncle. He looked so much like my father and spoke so much like him that I wanted to see him and talk to him about my father. I had not seen him for many years.

I remember so very well the day we drove to Tuscaloosa, spent the night in a motel, called my uncle, and told him we were in town. He did not know my wife or my children, but we told him we were there and that we wanted to see him.

He had not seen me since I was a child. I put on the best suit I had. My wife got all dressed up. We dressed our two boys to look their very best. We wanted everyone to look great.

When he walked through the doorway into the motel lobby, he looked so much like my father. I could not hold back the tears. Neither could he. As he spoke, he sounded so much like my father.

We hugged. We cried. He looked at us and he said we looked so nice. He repeated over and over how happy he was to see us and that he wanted us to get into his car so he could take us all around town, showing us off to everyone, telling everyone who we were, and explaining how we were related to him. That was quite a day. It was a precious day. It was a day I will always remember.

Joseph was filled with expectation at the thought of seeing his father. Every time he saw his brothers, he asked about his father. In chapter forty-three of Genesis, when Joseph was inquiring among his brethren concerning things at home, the Bible says in verse twenty-seven, *"And he asked them of their welfare, and said, Is your father well, the old man of whom ye spake? Is he yet alive?"* This was before Joseph revealed himself to his brethren.

When we come to chapter forty-five in the book of Genesis, just after Joseph made himself known to his brothers, the Bible says in verses two and three, *"And he wept aloud: and the Egyptians and the house of Pharaoh heard. And Joseph said unto his brethren, I am Joseph; doth my father yet live?"* He cried out, *"Doth my father yet live?"* His love for his father had burned in his heart for all those years.

The Word of God also says in Genesis 45:9, *"Haste ye, and go up to my father, and say unto him, Thus saith thy son Joseph, God hath made me lord of all Egypt: come down unto me, tarry not."*

In verse thirteen Joseph said, *"And ye shall tell my father of all my glory in Egypt, and of all that ye have seen; and ye shall haste and bring down my father hither."* He sent the chariots with his brothers and loaded them with all manner of good things. They got their father and brought him down to Egypt.

> *I choose to dwell on the good things, the blessed times, the precious moments in my life.*

Remember how the old man got on his face before God when he came to the southern border of the land of Canaan in Beersheba. He bowed himself before God and thanked

God that his son Joseph was alive. Jacob had not seen Joseph since he was a seventeen-year-old boy. Now Jacob was going to see his son.

As they traveled southward from the land of Canaan, through the desert, and into Egypt to the land of Goshen, Jacob sent Judah before him to prepare the way. An announcement was made that they had arrived and Joseph could get into his chariot and see his father. What a meeting!

I do not know how you look at things in the Bible, but I try to imagine every detail. I create a mental picture of how it happened. I put myself in the picture. I can see Joseph getting ready. I see him taking great pains to make sure he looked his best. He was going to see his father. I imagine how he mounted that chariot to make his way to his father.

Think of how Jacob felt as he looked at every person approaching, wondering if Joseph would look anything like he looked the last time he saw him. He wondered how he would speak and what was going on in his life. He longed to see Joseph.

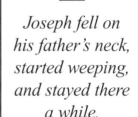

Joseph fell on his father's neck, started weeping, and stayed there a while.

The Word of God says in Genesis 46:29, *"And Joseph made ready his chariot, and went up to meet Israel his father, to Goshen, and presented himself unto him; and he fell on his neck, and wept on his neck a good while."* The Word of God does not say that one word was spoken. Joseph fell on his father's neck, started weeping, and stayed there a while. This was a precious moment in his life. What a beautiful thing!

WE SHOULD NEVER FORGET ALL THE GOOD AMONG THE BAD

This had not been an easy road for Joseph, and it had not been an easy road for Jacob. Since Joseph was sold into Egyptian bondage, he had not lived an easy life being separated from his family. However, Joseph was able to remember the good among the bad. God rewarded him with a precious moment in his lifetime when he could embrace his father. Before his father died, Joseph could put his arms around him, weep on his father's neck, and rejoice in all the good things that God had done for both of them. God gave an extension of years for them to be together.

As I look back across my life, I recall some things that caused great heartache. However, I choose to dwell on the good things, the blessed times, the precious moments in my life. I have thought so many times about my father and what he did for me. I remember the day he took me with him into the mountains of North Carolina and spent the day alone with me, talking with me, advising me, and counseling me as a young boy. I have never forgotten the things he said to me that day. He charged me not to waste my life. He went on to say that he had wasted his life and he did not want me to make the same mistake he had made. That was a precious moment for me, and I still carry it in my heart and mind after all these years. I cherish it as I bring it to mind time and time again.

> *The home is the training ground for life.*

I think about things that happened in my boyhood, experiences I enjoyed with my mother, brother, and two sisters. Some are humorous things we did together, funny things we laughed about. These are precious moments of my lifetime.

131

I remember the day a fine Christian man took the Bible and explained to me the way of salvation. That day I trusted the Lord Jesus Christ as my personal Savior. That day I became a child of God.

I think about the day I met the girl who would become my wife. I recall the day we married and the wonderful, precious moments we have had together. I think of how good God has been to me to give me such a faithful helpmeet.

I recall sitting in the hospital and waiting for the doctor to come to announce that my wife had given birth to our first son. I was so happy when I heard that God had given me a son. I can still see the doctor coming through the double doors in his hospital attire and announcing to me that I had a baby boy. I was a proud daddy of a new son. That was a precious moment.

I remember going back to the same hospital again a little less than three years later. I was preaching in a revival meeting. I was to be in the church at a certain time. Just before the revival service, my wife gave birth to our second son. The doctor came out and told me, and I was thrilled that I had another son. As he turned on his heels and walked toward the door, the doctor said, "There is one thing I forgot to tell you. He has his mother's nose." That was a precious moment.

There have been so many precious moments we have shared together as a family and many happy days those two boys have brought to my life. There have been so many happy days their mother has brought to my life.

I think about the day God called me to preach. These are precious moments. If we are not careful, we will get in some ditch of despair or discouragement and we will forget the good among the bad. I think we need to say by God's grace, "I'm not going to forget all the precious things God has done for me."

Can you still rejoice and praise God for the good things? Is His song still in your heart? Joseph waited a long time to be able to hug his father, put his arms around him, and weep on his father's neck. God gave him that precious moment in his life. Of all people, Christian people have so much for which to be thankful.

WE SHOULD HONOR OUR PARENTS

The Word of God says that Joseph stayed with his father for *"a good while."* Remember time after time Joseph asked about his father. We are reminded from this passage in the Bible that we should honor our parents.

In the book of Exodus chapter twenty, let us consider the fifth commandment given to us in verse twelve. The Bible says, *"Honour thy father and thy mother: that thy days may be long upon the land which the LORD thy God giveth thee."* This is God's command.

In Ephesians chapter six, the Bible says in verse one, *"Children, obey your parents in the Lord: for this is right."* Obedience is an action. God says that children are to obey their parents.

Ephesians 6:2 says, *"Honour thy father and mother."* Honor is an attitude. The action is obedience. You may be grown and gone from home and have a family of your own, but you are still obligated before God to honor your parents. You may not be under their authority, but you never escape the commandment to honor them. Your attitude toward your parents should be right.

I recommend to any young person who is a Christian not to even think about getting interested in a young man or young lady who does not honor his or her parents. If you marry someone who has never learned to honor his parents, that person will not show the respect that he has the God-given responsibility of showing to you.

The home is the training ground for life. If children do not learn in the home to honor their parents, they do not learn to respect and honor anyone else.

The Word of God says that we are to honor our parents. This is the clear teaching of the Word of God. It is a commandment. Joseph was true to God's command. He honored his father.

WE MUST DO WHAT WE CAN WHILE WE CAN

There is coming a day when the opportunity to do every good thing you want to do for someone will be gone. Either you will not be here to do it, or the person you intend to honor will not be around to receive your love. Do what you can while you can.

I heard an interview given on the news by a young man who was playing college football. His father was a professional football player who took his own life after killing his wife. It was a tragic story. The father had been a hero of professional athletes. But after he got out of professional sports, his life went to shambles. He killed his wife, and in the same night took his own life and left four children. His oldest son became a star football player in a major college in America, and the young man was being interviewed after receiving distinction for his outstanding performance on the field.

The reporter asked him, "If you could say one thing to your father, what would it be?" He broke down and started crying and said, "If I could say one thing, I would tell my dad that I love him."

Life is too precious and too short to live it the way so many people are living it, harboring things in their hearts that should not be there. If you are going to show love and tenderness to anyone, you had better do it while you can. If you have any good thing to say to someone to encourage him or express your love to him, you should do it now. Do what you can while you can.

I thank the Lord that God let Joseph and Jacob live so they could see one another and embrace. I am speaking purely from the human side of this story, thinking of the precious moment they shared together. We must do what we can while we can. Of all the things we do, there is nothing more important than trusting Christ as our Savior. Live your life in such a way that you leave no room for doubt concerning your faith in God.

There is not one person in hell who does not wish he had another opportunity to trust Christ. You have an opportunity. If you do not know the Lord Jesus Christ as your personal Savior, if you have never asked Him to forgive your sin and by faith received Him as your Savior, then you have an opportunity to do what you can while you can. You can trust Him as your Savior. It is a precious moment when you give your heart to the Lord Jesus Christ.

If you are a Christian and you know there are some things in your life you have neglected to do, then while you can do something about it and while the Holy Spirit is speaking to you, come before the

Is His song still in your heart?

Lord in prayer and say, "God, forgive me and cleanse me. Help me to be what I should be and do what I should do while there is time and while I can do it."

Chapter Eleven

GOD SHALL BE WITH YOU

acob, the father of Joseph, reached the time in life when he knew he would soon meet God. The days of his earthly journey were nearing their end. In this conversation between Joseph and Jacob, or Israel as Jacob is called, the Bible says in Genesis 48:21, *"And Israel said unto Joseph, Behold, I die: but God shall be with you, and bring you again unto the land of your fathers."*

Note the statement, *"God shall be with you."* This is one of those statements that is so full of power and meaning but is so easy to forget or overlook. *"God shall be with you."* Joseph made a vow to his father Jacob, a vow that he would keep. Joseph promised that when his father died, he would carry his body back to the land of Canaan for burial. It was the heart's desire of Jacob to be buried with Abraham and Isaac.

In Genesis chapter forty-eight, Joseph was called again to his father's side. The Bible says in Genesis 48:1, *"And it came to pass after these things, that one told Joseph, Behold, thy father is sick:*

and he took with him his two sons, Manasseh and Ephraim." Joseph took his sons to his dying father's side. Joseph wanted Jacob to do something for his sons. He wanted them to hear something from

Jacob says to his son Joseph, "God shall be with you."

their grandfather. He wanted them to experience something of what Jacob had experienced in his life. As this tender scene unfolded, Joseph took his place with his boys by his father's side. In the course of the conversation, Jacob looked at Joseph and said, "I want you to remember that God shall be with you."

I have been around at least two men in my life, both preachers of the gospel, who had a way of saying so much in very few words. One of them is Dr. Lee Roberson. His statements penetrated to the deepest part of the heart. His straightforward statements were used of God to get through.

Another man of few words was my first pastor, Dillard Hagan. Brother Hagan was my pastor when I answered the call to preach. I yielded to the desire that God had put in my heart to preach His Word, and I followed Brother Hagan around like a little puppy following his mother, listening to everything he said to people.

We had a certain lady in our church who was always in distress; at least she thought she was. On one occasion, she came to the pastor when I was standing by his side and started talking to him about all the things that had been going wrong in her life. Brother Hagan simply asked, "Has God forsaken you?" It shocked her. She said, "No." He said, "Then nothing is as bad as you think it is."

Think about the fact that God is with us. As Christians, we are never alone. We do not get into our automobiles alone. We do not go to our jobs alone. We do not live our lives in loneliness. Christ is our constant companion. We have divine companionship. Wherever we go, God goes with us.

In Deuteronomy chapter thirty-one, Moses was encouraging the people of God as he was about to die and leave Joshua in charge. The Bible says in Deuteronomy 31:6, *"Be strong and of a good courage, fear not, nor be afraid of them: for the LORD thy God, he it is that doth go with thee; he will not fail thee, nor forsake thee."* In other words Moses said, "I want you to realize that whatever you come up against, it is no match for the Lord. The Lord is going with you; He will not forsake you."

The Bible says in Hebrews 13:5, *"Let your conversation be without covetousness; and be content with such things as ye have: for he hath said, I will never leave thee, nor forsake thee."* So many times I am called on to be at someone's side when that person is facing some difficult circumstance in life. It might be just before undergoing serious surgery. It may be in a home after the news has come that a loved one has died. So many times I am called on to be at someone's side when that person must face great distress and trouble.

On many of those occasions, I have been able to give a Bible verse, just one verse, to provide encouragement that God is with us always. No matter what you are going through, consider Hebrews 13:5. The last part of the verse says, *"I will never leave thee, nor forsake thee."*

Jacob said to his son Joseph, *"God shall be with you."* There are many times when people I love have gone places without me, but I know they have never gone there without God. God was with us. There are times when I am away from

The presence of God makes life precious.

my wife, hundreds and hundreds of miles away, sometimes thousands of miles away, but God is always with her and He is always with me. What a comfort to know we have His companionship. He will never leave us or forsake us.

GOD'S PRESENCE

The Bible says in Genesis 48:1-2, *"And it came to pass after these things,..."* This was after Joseph and his father had their former conversation and Joseph had placed his hand under Jacob's thigh and had sworn to Jacob that when he died, he would take his body into Canaan. Joseph now was going to be called back to Jacob's side.

> *...that one told Joseph, Behold, thy father is sick: and he took with him his two sons, Manasseh and Ephraim. And one told Jacob, and said, Behold, thy son Joseph cometh unto thee: and Israel strengthened himself, and sat upon the bed.*

Notice how encouraged Jacob was to hear that Joseph was coming. My wife's grandfather was one of the godliest men I have ever known. He was a Baptist deacon for over half a century. He truly loved the Lord. On Sunday afternoons when I was pastoring in East Tennessee near where he lived, my wife and I would drive, if only for a short visit, to be with her grandparents. They lived on a little road called Mint Road in a small country community just outside of Maryville, Tennessee. They had rocking chairs on the porch. We would sit on the porch and look out across the fields. There we talked about the things of God. He would ask me how things had gone at church that morning, how many people came to Christ, and what God was doing. He wanted me to rehearse my entire message, tell him everything I preached about, and give him all the Scripture references. What grand conversations we had sitting on that porch together. He encouraged me so very much in the Lord. When he would come to hear me preach, he would cry and rejoice that a member of his family was preaching the gospel. He encouraged me so very much.

When Granddaddy became very ill, he was almost at the place where he did not recognize anyone in the hospital room. When I went to see him in that condition, one of his sons was standing by him and said, "Clarence is here." Suddenly, he raised up in the bed, opened his eyes, and started asking me how things had been going in the ministry. It was as if one of those conversations on the porch had come back to him. He wanted to know all about what God was doing in my life. He smiled and rejoiced and we prayed together. He seemed to gather just enough strength for that moment to reassure me that the path I was on was the best path and the thing I was doing with my life was the best thing. He thought I could be doing nothing better than what I was doing, serving the Lord.

I think this is the way it was when Joseph walked into Jacob's presence and someone announced that Joseph was there. I do not think the old man felt much like talking to anyone. As a matter of fact, death would have been a pleasant release. But when he heard the name Joseph, and he thought of that precious boy he had been away from for so long, the Bible says he *"strengthened himself, and sat upon the bed."* He was delighted to be able to talk to Joseph.

Verse three says, *"And Jacob said unto Joseph, God Almighty appeared unto me at Luz in the land of Canaan, and blessed me."* The first thing Jacob said was, "God came to me. God was with me." The presence of God makes life precious.

In John chapter fourteen, the Lord Jesus had been with His disciples and soon He was going to die. Physically He was going to be removed from their presence, but He said to them in verse sixteen, *"And I will pray the Father, and he shall give you another Comforter,..."* By this, He meant one just like the Lord Jesus. *"...that he may abide with you for ever."*

We believe in God the Father, God the Son, and God the Holy Spirit. We believe that God the Holy Spirit is co-equal, co-existent, eternally existent with God the Father and God the Son.

We believe that when God the Holy Spirit comes to live in us that it is God that comes to live in us. The Lord Jesus said in John 14:16-17,

> *And I will pray the Father, and he shall give you another Comforter, that he may abide with you for ever; even the Spirit of truth; whom the world cannot receive, because it seeth him not, neither knoweth him: but ye know him; for he dwelleth with you, and shall be in you.*

If you are a child of God, did you know that the eternal, Almighty God is living in you today? The same God who created this world, who made the human body, is in you. God Almighty is present with us today. He lives in us. Think of His presence.

How many times do we live our lives for days on end and never really recognize the fact that God is with us? I was reminded of this in a strong way after my wife had a serious surgery. I sat in the room with her, and she was so terribly sick. Finally, I had all I could take. Do you know what I did? I got tired of calling out and running to the nurses, and I asked God to help her. I should have done that to begin with. I told her, "I'm going to pray for you." I bowed my head and prayed for her. I said, "Lord, help her to get better. Help her to rest tonight. Help her to sleep and to recover from this."

Immediately, she went to sleep and did not have one bad episode all night. Oh, how we fail to realize that God is with us and we can call on Him anytime, any moment of the day.

When we ask the Lord to forgive our sin and by faith receive Christ as our Savior, the Bible says, *"But as many as received him, to them gave he power to become the sons of God, even to them that believe on his name"* (John 1:12). When we are born again, the Lord Jesus comes to live in us, and the Bible says He will dwell in us forever. We have His presence.

GOD'S POWER

Jacob said to Joseph, *"God shall be with you."* When we have His presence, we also have His power available to us. Let us think about Jacob's life. Jacob's life makes an interesting study. Jacob had certainly seen days of disappointment and heartache, but God by His power sustained him until his dying day.

In Genesis chapter forty-eight, Jacob rehearsed some of his testimony to Joseph. In verse seven he said, *"And as for me, when I came from Padan, Rachel died by me in the land of Canaan in the way."*

What he was saying was, "Joseph, I want to tell you something. When I came to Padan, your mother died there. We were so excited. She was expecting a baby. We were hoping it was another baby boy. That would give me twelve boys that would be blessed of God in a mighty way. When your mother was going to give birth to that baby boy, we were so full of joy. But when she was giving birth to your baby brother Benjamin I was right by her side as she died. It broke my heart. She is buried in Bethlehem."

Do you know what this old man was saying to his son? He was saying, "With the kind of life I have lived, I want you to know that it is God's power that has enabled me to continue. How do you think I felt, Son, when the boys came and told me that an evil beast had devoured you? How do you think I felt for all those years as I mourned for you? For more than twenty years, I mourned your death. God gave me strength. God's power enabled me."

> *There is no peace without resting in the Lord. The peace of God comes by placing our faith in Him.*

As I look back across my life, the only thing I can say is that I would not have made it had it not been for God's power. If God has taught me anything in life, He has taught me that nothing can be accomplished without Him. His Word is true. He said, *"Without me ye can do nothing"* (John 15:5).

You may be going through some things right now, and you wonder how you are going to make it through. Your heart is broken, and you are troubled. God wants you to see that He can prove Himself to you and prove that by His mighty power, He can enable you to do with your life what you should do.

GOD'S PEACE

In Genesis chapter forty-eight, Jacob talked about the birthright. Normally, the birthright went to the oldest. The birthright, by the way, involved two things. The birthright involved authority and it involved a double portion of inheritance. This birthright was going to be shared, not by the one we think would get the birthright, but by Joseph and Judah.

Jacob would say to Judah that Judah would share in the authority of the birthright. Joseph was going to share in the double inheritance of the birthright with his boys, Ephraim and Manasseh. Jacob actually said to Joseph, "You may have other children, but these two boys are going to be like mine. Of the twelve tribes of the nation of Israel, they are going to be like mine. They are going to share in the birthright."

Jacob was going to die. The Bible says in Genesis 48:21, *"And Israel said unto Joseph, Behold, I die:..."* He was not panicking. He said, "I am going to die, Son." God's grace enables a man to look at death like that.

Jacob continues, *"...but God shall be with you, and bring you again unto the land of your fathers."* That is peace. He said, "I do not have any human strength to do anything else. My life is totally out of my hands. I am going to die. But I want you to know that God is going to bring you into the land that He promised. Jacob had perfect peace, God's peace, that the Lord was in control and the Lord was going to work everything out perfectly. As I write these words, I have just hours ago left the bedside of one of our precious friends who is dying. She is going to be with her Savior and she has perfect peace. There is no fear. She is conscious. She is speaking clearly and resting completely in His care.

Many people today are worried. Do you know why? Because they fail to see that God's promises are true and they do not appropriate those promises to their lives. There is no peace without resting in the Lord. The peace of God comes by placing our faith in Him.

How many things today would you like to bring to the Lord and place in His hands and say, "Lord, here it is. I know You can take care of it like Jacob said, *'God shall be with you.'* Lord, here it is. I'm going to rest in You"? God can take care of our difficulty whether it be a person, a problem, a need, a family member, or a decision. The Bible says in Philippians 4:6-7, *"Be careful for nothing; but in every thing by prayer and supplication with thanksgiving let your requests be made known unto God. And the peace of God, which passeth all understanding, shall keep your hearts and minds through Christ Jesus."*

There are many times when people I love have gone places without me, but I know they have never gone there without God.

I have been a Christian for many years. When I look back across those years, I know that God has never failed me. Not one time has God ever failed to work everything out for my good and His glory. Why can we not simply trust Him with everything, knowing that the same God who never changes is going to be with us and take care of us just as He has always taken care of us?

He said, "Without me ye can do nothing" (John 15:5).

Jacob came to the place where he said, "Joseph, it's so good to see you and to see these boys God has given you. They are going to be like my boys now. I want you to know I am going to die, but God has given me peace. I want you to know the Lord is going to do exactly what He said He would do. I am going to leave everything in God's hands." When Jacob went to meet the Lord, he went in peace. We need to live our lives in peace, trusting the Lord Jesus and yielding to Him.

The Bible says, *"God shall be with you."* This is a precious truth. May we have the faith to believe this promise and claim it in our lives.

Chapter Twelve

WHEN DAD DIES

et us enter into the room with Joseph and his father Jacob, just as Jacob is going to meet God. The Bible gives us the story of the death and burial of Jacob in the closing part of chapter forty-nine and in chapter fifty of the book of Genesis. *Israel* was his name. God had used him mightily. Israel gave his blessing to his sons and went to be with God. He had lived a long distinguished life.

The Word of God tells the story in Genesis 50:1-13,

> *And Joseph fell upon his father's face, and wept upon him, and kissed him. And Joseph commanded his servants the physicians to embalm his father: and the physicians embalmed Israel. And forty days were fulfilled for him; for so are fulfilled the days of those which are embalmed: and the Egyptians mourned for him threescore and ten days. And when the days of his mourning were past, Joseph spake unto the house of Pharaoh,*

saying, If now I have found grace in your eyes, speak,
I pray you, in the ears of Pharaoh, saying, my father
made me swear, saying, Lo, I die: in my grave which
I have digged for me in the land of Canaan, there
shalt thou bury me. Now therefore let me go up, I pray
thee, and bury my father, and I will come again. And
Pharaoh said, Go up, and bury thy father, according
as he made thee swear. And Joseph went up to bury
his father: and with him went up all the servants of
Pharaoh, the elders of his house, and all the elders of
the land of Egypt, and all the house of Joseph, and
his brethren, and his father's house: only their little
ones, and their flocks, and their herds, they left in the
land of Goshen. And there went up with him both
chariots and horsemen: and it was a very great
company. And they came to the threshingfloor of
Atad, which is beyond Jordan, and there they
mourned with a great and very sore lamentation: and
he made a mourning for his father seven days. And
when the inhabitants of the land, the Canaanites, saw
the mourning in the floor of Atad, they said, This is a
grievous mourning to the Egyptians: wherefore the
name of it was called Abel-mizraim, which is beyond
Jordan. And his sons did unto him according as he
commanded them: for his sons carried him into the
land of Canaan, and buried him in the cave of the
field of Machpelah, which Abraham bought with the
field for a possession of a buryingplace of Ephron the
Hittite, before Mamre.

This was the death and burial of Jacob, the father of the men we
have come to know as those who began the tribes of Israel.

As a boy, I grew up in the little East Tennessee town of Maryville. It is a beautiful town not far from the Smoky Mountains. We lived on South Houston Street. Our house was on a big hill across the street from Maryville High School.

On Easter Sunday, 1963, my mother came across the street from our house, through the gate of the school, into a field where we were playing, and said to my brother and me, "Your dad died today." My mother was crying, and we started crying. This is a day I have never forgotten, the day my dad died.

When Jacob was dying, he called Joseph to his side and said, "I want you to make a promise to me that you will not bury me in Egypt. I want you to take my body out of Egypt back to Canaan to the cave of Machpelah that Abraham purchased and bury me there with Abraham and Isaac." Joseph placed his hand under the thigh of his father Jacob, as the custom was, and he swore to Jacob that when he died, this was exactly what he would do.

The Bible says in chapter forty-nine of the book of Genesis, as Jacob was dying, he called for his sons, and publicly before all of them, he rehearsed the oath that Joseph had made to him. The Bible says that when he died, they carried out his last request. Joseph got permission from Pharaoh to leave the land of Egypt after a period of seventy days of mourning to take his father's body from Egypt to Canaan to bury him.

> *Some of the greatest things God teaches us are taught during the days when we deal with the deaths of ones we love.*

I can imagine the funeral procession leaving Egypt. It was not just Joseph and his brothers with the body of Jacob. A great host of Egyptians and chariots of Egypt accompanied them. More than likely there were military personnel from Egypt. This great host of people traveled from Egypt to the burying place of Jacob.

151

When they came near to the burial place, they stopped for seven days, beyond Jordan at the threshing floor of Atad, and mourned there. All of the Egyptians stayed behind in that place, and only the sons of Jacob took Jacob's body to the cave of Machpelah in Hebron and buried it there.

After they buried their father, no doubt they saw the familiar surroundings of their boyhood and remembered the lives they had lived before they went down into Egypt during the time of famine. Then they returned to Egypt to be with their families and herds. Jacob was dead and buried.

Some of the greatest things God teaches us are taught during the days when we deal with the deaths of ones we love. Some of the most lasting impressions the Lord makes on our hearts are made as we contemplate death.

In this beautiful story, Jacob's sons carried out their father's last request. It is a human story of a death in a family. It is a story of love and hope. It is a story that I believe God can use to speak to all of us about some of the most serious matters in life.

THE COMING OF DEATH TO ALL OF US

If the Lord Jesus Christ does not come soon, we are all going to die. Jacob was 147 years old, but he died. The Bible says, *"And as it is appointed unto men once to die"* (Hebrews 9:27).

When Jacob died, Joseph was with him and he fell on his father's body and wept. Joseph must have thought of many things. With the responsibility he had been given in Egypt, he had been able, for the last seventeen years, to go to his father's side for counseling, comfort, and encouragement. Those days were over.

Once death comes, a final curtain is drawn. Let us consider what God said in Genesis chapter three when Adam sinned against God and

sin entered into the bloodstream of all humanity through our first parents. God came in the cool of the day, walking in the Garden of Eden and pronounced this curse. The Bible tells us in Genesis 3:14-15,

> *And the LORD God said unto the serpent, Because thou hast done this, thou art cursed above all cattle, and above every beast of the field; upon thy belly shalt thou go, and dust shalt thou eat all the days of thy life: and I will put enmity between thee and the woman, and between thy seed and her seed; it shall bruise thy head, and thou shalt bruise his heel.*

This is the first promise given in the Bible foretelling that our Savior would come into the world and be born of a virgin. The Bible says in verses sixteen through nineteen,

> *Unto the woman he said, I will greatly multiply thy sorrow and thy conception; in sorrow thou shalt bring forth children; and thy desire shall be to thy husband, and he shall rule over thee. And unto Adam he said, Because thou hast hearkened unto the voice of thy wife, and hast eaten of the tree, of which I commanded thee, saying, Thou shalt not eat of it: cursed is the ground for thy sake; in sorrow shalt thou eat of it all the days of thy life; thorns also and thistles shall it bring forth to thee; and thou shalt eat the herb of the field; in the sweat of thy face shalt thou eat bread, till thou return unto the ground; for out of it wast thou taken: for dust thou art, and unto dust shalt thou return.*

God said, "You are going to die." If you could put yourself in Adam's place, you would realize the significance of this statement. This was news to Adam. Adam was created by God. He had lived in a dispensation of innocence. There was no sin in the world. He could live forever like that. There was no reason to die. There was nothing to bring about death. The earth was beautiful and perfect. It was exactly as God had made it. There was nothing to harm or hinder. There was no curse. But then sin came and God drew the bottom line on sin in verse nineteen of chapter three of Genesis. God said, "The bottom line to all of this is very simple; you are going to die." This is what sin does. It brings forth death.

> *A human tragedy came to his household. Yet there was not one thing they could do to bring him back. His voice had been silenced. Their father was dead.*

People speak often about living longer. Of course, I want to live just as long as I possibly can. I think people who get in a hurry to die and start talking about it have something wrong with them. Yet, any serious-minded human being must come to grips with the fact that he is going to die. Life expectancy has risen twenty years from two generations ago. This is great, but another statement needs to be added, "We're still going to die." It is going to happen.

Jacob lived a noble life, but he died. A human tragedy came to his household. His family felt the awful burden of death, and tears of sorrow ran down their cheeks as they embraced the lifeless body of their father and sobbed with great hurt. Yet there was not one thing they could do to bring him back. His voice had been silenced. Their father was dead.

May God help us to be wise enough to see that the Bible is true and to realize that we are not going to live on this earth forever. We are going to die. Death is coming.

THE CONQUERING OF DEATH

Imagine how awful death would be if it could not be conquered, if it could not be defeated. I would hate to think that death would always keep its icy grip upon us and cause us to live in constant fear.

As Joseph fell over in the bed on the body of his father and wept, his father was already gone. The hardest thing about my father's death was getting used to the fact that he was no longer here. Even though we did not see as much of him as children normally see their father, I had to come to grips with the fact that I could no longer talk to him, that I would not hear his voice here again.

God has a way of using death to make life more precious to us. My father's body was placed into the grave, and we stood there gathered around the casket looking down into the grave. It had been raining. It was a sad day. It really gripped my heart. I watched with a broken heart as they lowered his body into that muddy grave.

Notice the last statement God makes in Genesis 49:33, *"And when Jacob had made an end of commanding his sons, he gathered up his feet into the bed, and yielded up the ghost,..."* God could have put a period there, but there is no period because that is not when it stops. That is where earthly vision stops. But the Bible is an eternal Book written by an eternal God who sees everything, so the next expression is given, *"...and was gathered unto his people."*

The Bible is an eternal Book written by an eternal God who sees everything, so the next expression is given, "...and was gathered unto his people."

Beyond the grave, beyond death, beyond this life, beyond the cold, lifeless body left behind, there is an eternal life with Jesus Christ for

those who have trusted Him as their personal Savior. It is real, just as real as what we see. Death has been conquered through the power of the Lord Jesus Christ.

Consider John chapter eleven and the statement our Lord made to the sisters of Lazarus. This may not mean as much to you today as it will someday, but I guarantee you that someday when you deal with death, it will be very precious to you. It will give you hope, comfort, and consolation that nothing else on earth will give you. The Bible says in John 11:19-27,

> *And many of the Jews came to Martha and Mary, to comfort them concerning their brother. Then Martha, as soon as she heard that Jesus was coming, went and met him: but Mary sat still in the house. Then said Martha unto Jesus, Lord, if thou hadst been here, my brother had not died. But I know, that even now, whatsoever thou wilt ask of God, God will give it thee. Jesus saith unto her, Thy brother shall rise again. Martha saith unto him, I know that he shall rise again in the resurrection at the last day. Jesus said unto her, I am the resurrection, and the life: he that believeth in me, though he were dead, yet shall he live: and whosoever liveth and believeth in me shall never die. Believest thou this? She saith unto him, Yea, Lord: I believe that thou art the Christ, the Son of God, which should come into the world.*

The Lord Jesus said, "He is dead yet he shall live." He is talking about conquering death. In I Corinthians 15:51-57 God says,

> *Behold, I shew you a mystery; We shall not all sleep, but we shall all be changed, in a moment, in the twinkling of an eye, at the last trump: for the trumpet shall sound, and the dead shall be raised*

incorruptible, and we shall be changed. For this corruptible must put on incorruption, and this mortal must put on immortality. So when this corruptible shall have put on incorruption, and this mortal shall have put on immortality, then shall be brought to pass the saying that is written, Death is swallowed up in victory. O death, where is thy sting? O grave, where is thy victory? The sting of death is sin; and the strength of sin is the law. But thanks be to God, which giveth us the victory through our Lord Jesus Christ.

Jesus Christ has already paid the penalty we owe for our sin. Someone said death is like a bee buzzing around threatening to sting you, but he cannot sting you because his stinger is gone. Death will threaten to sting you, but it cannot sting you if you have been born again. If you have trusted in Jesus Christ, He has taken death's sting for you. He has suffered your penalty on the cross of Calvary. Death has been conquered through our Lord Jesus.

In other words, God has given us the miraculous freedom not to fear death. We can go on living life to the fullest knowing that someday we are going to pass from this life through the door of death into eternity to be with God forever. I have no way of knowing how many gravesides you have been to or how many of your loved ones have died. But I am sure you will agree that it means more than words can tell to stand at a casket and look into the face of someone you love and know you are going to meet again in heaven.

It means more than words can tell to stand at a casket and look into the face of someone you love and know you are going to meet again in heaven.

The Concern for the Living

Joseph was good to his father. He loved him. When Jacob was 130 years old, he came into Egypt, and for the next 17 years Joseph got to be with his father. I believe he made every minute count. But I think that day when Joseph threw himself on his father's body and wept, he must have thought about so much more he would like to have done.

> *Imagine how awful death would be if it could not be conquered, if it could not be defeated.*

Some people never speak to their loved ones and when their loved ones die, they wish to God that they could live it all over. Then it is too late. Think of looking at a loved one's lifeless body and knowing there is no time left to make things right. The concern we need is for the living.

It will help us to imagine for a moment that everyone in our sphere of love is gone. What should we have said and done while there was time? Whatever it is, we must do it while there is time. Life is so short. Precious time is passing.

When my mother and I would argue, we would both cry. Then she would say, "Life is too short for this, Honey. Life is too short for this." She was right.

I remember a certain phone call I received from a man who identified himself as a funeral director. He asked, "Is this Reverend Sexton?" I really do not like to be called "Reverend," but I understood what he wanted.

He said, "I'm trying to find a Baptist preacher."

I said, "You found one."

He replied, "Someone has died in this city, and the family says the deceased was a Baptist and they want a Baptist pastor to conduct the funeral. Would you be willing to do it?" I have had many requests like that through the years and, of course, I am happy to help if I can.

I made arrangements with the man to be at the funeral home, and I said, "Before you go, tell me who is left. Sons? Daughters? Is there someone who needs our attention?" I thought in that moment that there is absolutely nothing according to the Bible that can be done for the deceased. But there is much that can be done for the living.

You may not have been called to a funeral home, but there are people living around you that you need to be concerned about. There are mothers, fathers, brothers, sisters, sons, and daughters who need to hear of the love of the Lord Jesus Christ. Determine that you are going to get out and do something to show concern for the living.

Chapter Thirteen

THE JOURNEY OF JOSEPH'S BONES "GOD WILL..."

Faith in God is not believing that God can, but that God will. In our study of the life of Joseph, I trust we have seen Christlikeness in him. As others behold us, may they see Christ in us.

The Word of God records the closing of Joseph's life on earth. The Bible says in Genesis 50:24-25, *"And Joseph said unto his brethren, I die: and God will surely visit you, and bring you out of this land unto the land which he sware to Abraham, to Isaac, and to Jacob. And Joseph took an oath of the children of Israel, saying, God will surely visit you, and ye shall carry up my bones from hence."*

Joseph repeated in his dying statement, *"God will surely visit you."* His faith in God never wavered. Where is your faith? Is it in the Lord Jesus Christ?

Egypt was full of faith in Joseph's day, but not true faith. People believed in idols, strange gods, false gods. But a real

faith was alive in Joseph's heart. The object of living faith is the Lord Jesus Christ. Because he believed the Lord, he said, *"God will surely visit you."*

Joseph was 110 years old. When he was about to die, he said to his brethren, "I want you to know something. God is going to do what He said He would do. What God said to Abraham, to Isaac, and to Jacob, God will surely do. I know He will. God is going to perform what He said He would do."

In Genesis chapter twelve, God spoke to Abraham. The Bible says in verses one through three,

> *Now the LORD had said unto Abram, Get thee out of thy country, and from thy kindred, and from thy father's house, unto a land that I will shew thee: and I will make of thee a great nation, and I will bless thee, and make thy name great; and thou shalt be a blessing: and I will bless them that bless thee, and curse him that curseth thee: and in thee shall all families of the earth be blessed.*

God made a promise to Abraham. He confirmed that covenant again to Abraham. Joseph said to his brethren, "I have faith to believe that the Lord will keep His Word. So when you leave here, I want you to take my bones with you."

Joseph did not make the same request that his father had made to him. Remember that Jacob said, "When I die, I want my body to be taken out immediately." Jacob made Joseph make an oath to him. When Jacob died, Joseph stayed true to his father's word and carried his body to be buried in Canaan.

Joseph knew that his brethren were not going to be able to immediately take his body and transport it to the land of Canaan, the

Land of Promise. But he said, "When you do leave, take my bones with you."

It is interesting to follow the journey of Joseph's bones. In the book of Exodus, God proved to the nation of Egypt that He was the true and living God. God demonstrated to the Egyptians that He was the God of all power. Through the judgment God brought upon Egypt, their power was broken, their gods were seen to be false, and the Lord was victorious. God proved Himself. Their power, their yoke on God's people, was broken. God's people were set free.

The Word of God says in the book of Exodus that the children of Israel remembered Joseph's words to them and they took his bones. With everything else they carried out of Egypt, they carried the bones of Joseph. The Bible says in Exodus 13:19, *"And Moses took the bones of Joseph with him: for he had straitly sworn the children of Israel, saying, God will surely visit you; and ye shall carry up my bones away hence with you."*

When God's people were in that fiery furnace of Egyptian persecution for those 430 years, their hearts were aglow, their hope lived, and their faith existed on the very promise of God believed by Joseph and others. God would visit them and bring them out. With surety and absolute assurance, Joseph said, *"God will surely visit you."*

> *Through the judgment God brought upon Egypt, their power was broken, their gods were seen to be false, and the Lord was victorious.*

When they finally got into the Land of Promise, Joshua took responsibility for the bones of Joseph. Joshua, as you may know, was of the tribe of Ephraim, the tribe coming from the loins of Joseph. No doubt Joshua took keen delight in taking care of this responsibility himself because Joseph was his grandfather from many generations back. The Bible says in Joshua 24:32, *"And the bones of Joseph, which the children of Israel brought up out of Egypt, buried they in Shechem, in a parcel of ground which Jacob bought of the sons of Hamor the father of Shechem for an hundred pieces of silver: and it became the inheritance of the children of Joseph."*

In reality, death is only a possibility; the Second Coming of Christ is a certainty.

The story of the bones of Joseph is a story of faith, not simply a story of human interest. Here was a man in a strange land surrounded by people who did not know the Lord. He worked among people who did not know the Lord. When he was 110 years old, Joseph still believed with all his heart in the true and living God and in his dying breath said, "I want you to know that my faith has never waned. I want you to know that God will do what He said." His faith was alive. His faith was strong. He spoke of it to his brethren.

What about your faith? What do you believe about God? You may go to church where they believe the Bible and where they talk about the fact that the object of our faith must be the Lord Jesus Christ, and yet your faith may not be real.

Hebrews chapter eleven is a chapter about faith. The Christian life should declare that God is real. If you are a Christian, your life should be making that statement. If you are a husband and a father, the statement to your wife and children should be that "God is real." By the very life you live, your life should be a billboard that states, "God is real."

If you are a wife and a mother, your life should be a sign that says, "God is real. I want you to know, children, I want you to know, husband, God is real." Your life should be a demonstration of the reality of God.

The Bible says in Hebrews 11:6, *"But without faith it is impossible to please him: for he that cometh to God must believe that he is,..."* Let us stop here for a moment. Do you believe that God is eternal? Do you believe that He is God?

You may say, "I don't have the faith someone else has, but I have faith. I believe in the Lord." The Word of God says in Hebrews 11:6 that if you come to the Lord Jesus, you *"...must believe that he is, and that he is a rewarder of them that diligently seek him."*

Joseph took the promise that God had made, and he put his faith in God's Word. We have so much more today than Joseph had. We do not have a greater God. God is almighty. But think how much more opportunity we have to know about our Lord Jesus Christ and His death, burial, and resurrection, how much more we know because of the completed written revelation of the Word of God to us. Think about how much more God has given us and how strong our faith should be.

The Lord Jesus never changes. Our faith has found a resting place in Him. Men will fail. Things will happen that will disappoint us deeply, but God never fails. He never changes. He never varies. He stays constant. He says of Himself in Malachi 3:6, *"I change not."*

Things will happen that will disappoint us deeply, but God never fails.

As we think about men and we think about God, let us notice what God's Word says in Romans 11:33. The Bible says, *"O the depth of the riches both of the wisdom and knowledge of God! how unsearchable are his judgments, and his ways past finding out!"* In other words, there are human limitations that we face. We can never plunge the depth and know all about God and what He is doing. His ways are past finding out.

We have limitations, but God is not limited. He never changes. He is eternal. Our faith can rest in Him. We must not put our faith in men. The object of our faith must be the Lord Jesus Christ. You and I are going to live very disappointed lives if we do not get this settled. We must look to the Lord Jesus Christ every day. We all have problems. We all have limitations. But God never changes.

> *Egypt was full of faith in Joseph's day, but not true faith.*

Think about Joseph and his brethren. Think about Joseph and his problems in Egypt. After all that Joseph went through, he said as a 110-year-old man, "God never changes. God will do what He says. He will never vary. When God gets around to doing what He said, I want you to take my bones and carry them out of here." He had faith to believe God.

SALVATION BY FAITH

Let us consider what God will do in the matter of salvation. God will receive anyone who will come to Him by faith to be saved. He will not cast anyone out. John 6:37 says, *"All that the Father giveth me shall come to me; and him that cometh to me I will in no wise cast out."* There is no one so hell-bound and lost, so wretched, so far from God, that when that person turns to the Lord, the Lord will not receive him unto Himself. God will save him, bring him into His family, and make him a child of God. This is what God will do.

Do you remember when you were saved? Do you remember when you put your faith in the Lord Jesus Christ and trusted Him for salvation? Did you recognize that you were a lost sinner and without Christ you could not go to heaven? Did you believe you would die and go to hell? When you confessed your sin and asked the Lord to forgive you, and by faith trusted Jesus Christ as your Savior, God did what He said He would do.

We are children of the Devil by nature; we must become children of God by faith. You may be religious or have some church affiliation. You may believe there is a God and believe parts of the Bible, but the only way to be saved is to trust Jesus Christ and Christ alone for salvation.

Salvation is through Jesus Christ and Him alone. When you come to trust only Jesus Christ, the Lord promised He would save you. The Lord Jesus said in John 14:6, *"I am the way, the truth, and the life: no man cometh unto the Father, but by me."* What will God do in the matter of salvation? God will save all of those who come to Him by faith.

LIVING BY FAITH

Let us look at what God will do in the matter of our daily living. Faith does not stop when we are saved. This is the beginning of the faith life. Faith must be exercised each day in the Christian life.

The only thing many know about Christianity is an experience they had with the Lord. If someone asks you if you are a Christian, do you only answer, "Yes, I was saved," followed by the time and place you received the Lord Jesus as your Savior? That should not be the only thing to talk about in our Christian lives. I know that I am a Christian, not only because there was a day and hour when I gave my heart to the Lord Jesus. I know I am a Christian because God has been treating me like one of His children ever since that day. I know it. There will be evidences that we are His children.

Joseph lived to be 110 years old, but we met him in the Bible when he was 17. He had faith in the Lord. His father had told him about the Lord, about the promise of God to his father Isaac and his

grandfather Abraham, and Joseph chose to believe the same promise. We met Joseph as a teenager. All of those years he kept his faith in the Lord.

I have been a Christian for many years. I can tell you that God has kept His Word to me. The Lord never varies; He never changes. Joseph could say to his brethren with absolute assurance, "God will do what He said He would do," because he lived by faith. It is just that simple.

I have seen failure, but I have never seen Jesus Christ fail. I have had problems, but I have never had a problem with Jesus Christ. He is perfect. What will God do in the matter of our daily living? He will take care of us.

I want to recommend something to you. No matter how young you are or how old you are, if you are a Christian, if you know you have trusted the Lord as your Savior, you should be growing in your Christian life day by day. The Lord should be more real to you today than He was a year ago or six months ago

DYING BY FAITH

The day of the Christian's death will be the greatest day he ever lives. It is the day he will see the Lord Jesus Christ. In reality, death is only a possibility; the Second Coming of Christ is a certainty.

Consider what Joseph said in Genesis chapter fifty. The Bible says in verse twenty-four, *"And Joseph said unto his brethren, I die."* He simply said, *"I die."* That is it.

I remember hearing Cathy Rice, the wife of Dr. Bill Rice, say that the day Dr. Bill Rice died, he got a little sick and went into the bedroom and sat across the bed and said to his wife, "Princess, this is the end of the trail. I'll see you in heaven." And he died. He just died. Joseph said, "I'm dying. When you get out of here, take my bones and bury them in the land of Canaan."

What will God do for you in the day of dying? God will be with you to take you to glory when you take your last breath. It might be on a battlefield. It might be on a highway. The issues of death are in God's hands. It might be anywhere, but whenever it comes and wherever it comes, the Lord Jesus has promised to be with you. *"He that is our God is the God of salvation; and unto GOD the Lord belong the issues from death"* (Psalm 68:20).

When we take our last breath, God has promised to take us to be with Him. Tender hands will come and take our bodies to be prepared for burial, but we will not be in that body. We will be with Christ because that is what God will do in the day of dying for His children. God's Word says, *"Absent from the body,...present with the Lord"* (II Corinthians 5:8).

We need faith to live. *"But without faith it is impossible to please him"* (Hebrews 11:6). We need faith in the dying hour to be able to look our Lord in the face and to know that He has never failed us. I have no reason to believe He is going to fail me in that hour. He is always faithful. In all this, He has kept His Word. I have not always kept mine, but He has always kept His. I have every reason to believe, from what I know about the Bible, what I have experienced in the past, and what He has given me of

> *I have seen failure, but I have never seen Jesus Christ fail.*

His Word, that when I come to die, He will take me with Him forever. There is rest and peace in trusting Him. Oh, how much there is to learn from the life of Joseph.